# THE VEGETABLE, FRUIT & NUT COOKBOOK

A collection of 400 meatless meals
from cherry and beetroot soup to vegetable curry
that reveal the inexhaustible variety
of vegetarian cuisine.

# THE VEGETABLE, FRUIT & NUT COOKBOOK

## A Vegetarian's Treasure Chest of Culinary Delights

by
Winifred Graham

**THORSONS PUBLISHERS LIMITED**
**Wellingborough, Northamptonshire**

First published 1980

ISBN 0 7225 0498 5 (hardback)
ISBN 0 7225 0643 0 (paperback)
Design, illustrations and photographs by Stonecastle Graphics

Photoset by Specialised Offset Services Limited, Liverpool
and printed and bound in Great Britain by
Butler & Tanner Ltd., Frome, Somerset

# Contents

# Foreword

Many people who have no intention of becoming totally committed vegetarians are now enjoying regular meals that do not rely on meat or fish, and the realization is growing that for healthy hearts, slim figures, good digestion, better nutritional balance, economy *and* variety, more meals without animal foods are a valuable habit.

And yet the urge to be free of the butcher's counter (especially after seeing the price of lamb chops!) often lasts no longer than the next dish of macaroni cheese. For what meatless dishes, apart from such familiar standbys as cauliflower cheese or omelettes, can you serve up with the confidence that they will be satisfying and acceptable to a conservative guest or carnivorous family?

This book provides a host of answers. Winifred Graham has collected her recipes slowly and with care. This is not cooking for cranks but for the person who likes good food and who wants to widen their repertoire of non-meat dishes.

The health benefits of cutting down meat consumption should not be underestimated. As Editor of *Here's Health* magazine, I receive many letters a year from people who have found that eating more meals without meat (but with lots of other natural foods) brought health improvements they had not expected: better digestion, improved skin condition, stable weight, and so on. Of course, everyone is different, but there is a convincing body of evidence that a gentle shift towards fewer meat meals would benefit most of us. Why?

To begin with, nutritionists say that the average person eats far too much fat – especially animal fat and they would like us to eat more plant food. Our overload of fat (and even the leanest meat carries a high, if invisible, portion of it) gives us too many calories for the unenergetic style of modern life. At the same time, it leaves us no appetite for the plant foods that are rich sources of vitamins, minerals and all-important roughage. And although proof has not been established, high animal fat diets are increasingly linked with heart disease, high blood-pressure, thrombosis, breast tumours, obesity and cancer of the bowel.

Secondly, meat and fish are far more concentrated foods than fruit and vegetables. This means that you get more calories in less weight of food, for the reason that animal foods contain little fibre and less water. Although we all need protein, which meat is high in, there are plenty of other sources. In any case, most of us eat more protein than we need. When we overload ourselves with protein, our bodies have to work harder at digestion and the excretion of waste products. Eating habits that include less concentrated foods are helpful in slimming or in keeping slim; meals are easier to digest; and the foods contain a high quantity of fibre, the essential 'wrapping' for waste products if our bodies are to process and get rid of them efficiently and quickly.

Thirdly, animals foods are the main causes of food poisoning. Anyone who is at all vulnerable to this can avoid it to a great extent by using fewer meat and fish ingredients. This is especially important for those without a refrigerator – when camping or living in a bedsitter, for example. It is also important for the person who lives alone who may tend to use up a single purchase of meat at a dangerously slow rate.

Finally, there are the economic facts. As Katherine Whitehorn wrote in her classic book *Cooking in a Bedsitter*, if vegetables cost 30p a pound, we consider them expensive; if meat costs 30p a pound, we consider it cheap. Moral: eat more vegetables. Fruit in season is cheap too. As for nuts, although they may not seem to be cheap pound for pound, few foods cram more nourishment into such a small space – including the most valuable forms of fat and plenty of roughage. In fact, a two to three ounce serving of nuts works out cheaper than most meats.

These, then, are the arguments behind this book, although Winifred Graham's recipes need no justification. They prove that eating without meat is no penance. And isn't it nice to know that every one of these enjoyable meals is actually doing you good?

MIRIAM POLUNIN
Editor *Here's Health* magazine

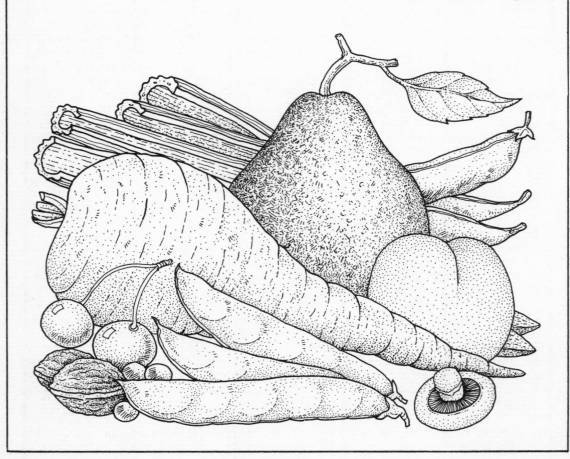

# British/American Conversions

## Liquid Measure Equivalents

| British | American |
|---------|----------|
| 1 teaspoonful | $1\frac{1}{2}$ teaspoonsful |
| 1 tablespoonful | $1\frac{1}{4}$ tablespoonsful |
| 1 pint (20 fl. oz.) | $1\frac{3}{4}$ pints |

## Cup Measures

A British standard measuring cupful contains 10 fl. oz. (275ml).

An American standard measuring cupful contains 8 fl. oz. (225ml).

## Ingredient Equivalents

| British | American |
|---------|----------|
| Biscuits | Cookies or crackers |
| Butter/margarine | Shortening |
| Demerara sugar | Brown or Turbinado sugar |
| Double cream | Heavy cream |
| Scones | Biscuits |
| Single cream | Light cream |
| Sultanas | White raisins |
| Vegetable fats | Soft shortening |

## Note
Nutter is a vegetable fat, but any non-animal fat may be used.

# Chapter One
# SOUPS

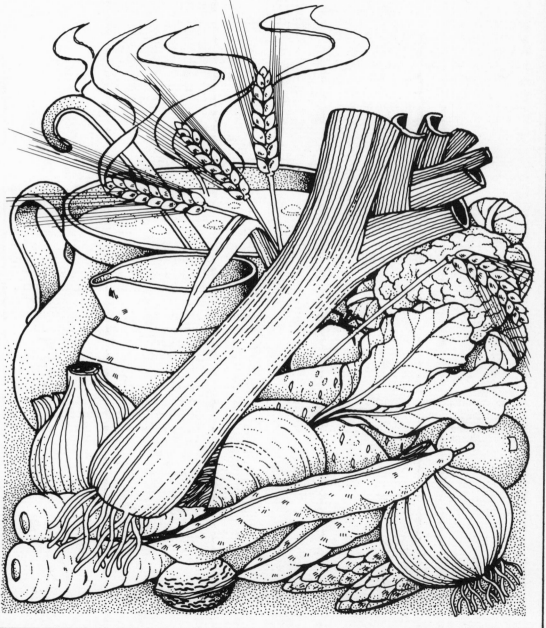

## STOCKS

Vegetable stocks may be made from practically any vegetable. Onions or chicory should be avoided, though, because their flavour is too strong; potatoes make a cloudy stock, and beetroots colour the stock too vividly. But otherwise, anything goes.

A pound (450g) to 1½ pints (825ml) water are about the right proportions. Boil up quickly and then simmer from one to two hours. Wash all the vegetables but do not peel them. Add all outside leaves.

Unless otherwise stated, quantities are given for six people.

## BORTSCH

3 fair-sized raw beetroots
3 carrots
3 shallots
½ a small cabbage (optional)
2 leeks
3 tablespoonful oil, not butter
1 qt. (1¼l) vegetable stock
¼ pt. (150ml) soured cream
2 tablespoonsful lemon juice
2 teaspoonsful sugar
1 large bay leaf
Salt to taste

Clean and peel the vegetables and cut all except one beetroot into small pieces. Heat half the oil and cook the vegetables in it for a few minutes, stir well and cook for a further 8 minutes. Pour in the stock and cook until the vegetables are tender then add the bay leaf, lemon juice, salt and sugar and cook for a few minutes. Sieve the mixture. Grate the remaining beetroot into the soup. Top with a blob of sour cream as it is being served.

This next soup is generally known as Soupe Parmentier but is also called Clear Potato Soup, though it is not really clear because potatoes always cloud a soup slightly.

## CLEAR POTATO SOUP

½ lb (225g) potatoes
1½ pt. (825ml) vegetable stock or water
2 large carrots
1 medium onion
A few pieces of celery
A few outer cabbage leaves
2 oz. (50g) butter or oil
1 teaspoonful yeast extract
¼ teaspoonful marjoram
Salt and pepper to taste

Wash the vegetables, cut the cabbage leaves into very thin strips. Scrape or peel the rest of the vegetables and cube them. Melt 1 oz. (25g) of the fat in a saucepan. Add the carrots and cook for a minute, then add the celery and lastly the onion and cabbage. Cook over a very low heat for 10 minutes without water, stirring often so that the vegetables do not stick to the pan and burn. Add the potatoes and cook for about 5 minutes. Now add ½ pt. (275ml) of water and cook until the vegetables are nearly tender. Then add the rest of the stock, the fat, salt and pepper, yeast extract and marjoram and cook for about a minute or a little longer if the vegetables are not tender. Croutons of fried brown bread go well with this soup.

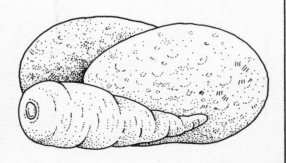

# CLEAR VEGETABLE BROTH

1½ pt. (825ml) stock
½ oz. (12g) butter or margarine
1 teaspoonful yeast extract
1 small bay leaf
A few sprigs of parsley
Salt to taste

Boil all the ingredients except the parsley together for about 20 minutes. Add finely-chopped parsley just before serving.

# CREAM OF CELERY SOUP

2 pt. (1¼l) stock with plenty of celery water in it
1 large head of celery
1 teaspoonful celery salt
1 teaspoonful Marmite (or similar)
2 oz. (50g) flour
2 oz. (50g) nutter
Chopped celery leaves

Wash the celery and cut into ½-inch strips. Peel the onion and cube it. Melt ½ oz. (15g) of the fat in a saucepan, add the celery and cook for 5 minutes, stirring often. This helps to bring out the delicious flavour. Add ½ pt. (275ml) of stock and cook until tender. Melt the rest of the nutter in the soup pan, add the onion and cook until golden, then stir in the flour and cook and stir for 5 minutes. Add the rest of the stock and cook until thickened, then lower the hear and cook for 15-20 minutes. Add the Marmite, celery salt and chopped celery leaves. Simmer for about 5 minutes and then serve. Cream or rich milk may be used instead of part of the stock to make a richer soup. The celery may be liquidized if preferred.

# CHERRY AND BEETROOT SOUP

8 small beets
30 stoned morello cherries
3 cloves
1 tablespoonful finely minced onion
1½ tablespoonsful clear honey
Juice of 1 lemon or lime
Salt

Scrub the beets and either grate or slice them very thinly. Boil them in 1 qt. (1¼l) water with the onion. Cook for 25 minutes, then strain but do not press the beets. Add the salt to the liquid. Simmer the cherries in ½ pt. (275ml) water with the cloves; cook for 10 minutes. Add the honey and lemon or lime juice to the first mixture, then mix the cherries and their liquid with the beet juice. Chill well and serve with some soured cream on each helping.

## CREAM OF BROCCOLI SOUP

1½ measuring cupsful cooked broccoli, chopped
2 teaspoonsful minced onion
½ green pepper, chopped
2 tablespoonsful butter, nutter or margarine
A little milk
½ cupful soured cream
½ teaspoonful curry powder
Salt and cayenne pepper

*Sauté* the onion and green pepper in the fat. When they are soft, *purée* them, adding a little water if needed, then add a little milk and the cream. Mix in the curry powder and taste for seasonings. Make to the right consistency with milk. Serve garnished with a blob of cream and chives. This soup may be served hot or cold. It has a much more delicate flavour than soup made from cauliflower. Garnish with chives or soured cream.

Add the turmeric and blend the two *purées* together. Cut a little dill with sharp scissors or use about 1 level teaspoonful of basil. Thin this thick *purée* with cream. Garnish with chopped chives, parsley or spring onions. The turmeric gives this delicious and sophisticated soup a lovely golden colour.

## CREAM OF CORN SOUP

4-6 ears of sweet corn
Butter, nutter or margarine
¼ cupful diced onion, or shallots
¼ cupful green pepper
½ teaspoonful turmeric
Fresh dill or basil
Salt and cayenne pepper
½ pt. (275ml) thin cream

Cook the corn and then score the centres of the kernels to release the milk, cut the corn from the cobs and scrape the ears carefully. Do this over a bowl so that nothing is lost. *Purée* the corn in an electric blender with a little added milk – warm is best. It will be necessary to sieve it afterwards because the blender leaves little sharp skins. Melt the fat and *sauté* the onions and green pepper in it and then *purée* with a little milk if needed.

## CREAM OF SPINACH SOUP

1½ lb (675g) spinach
1 chopped onion
2 tablespoonsful vegetarian fat
1 teaspoonful sugar
1 teaspoonful dried tarragon
¼ pt. (150ml) thin cream
Chopped parsley for garnish

Wash the spinach well, using warm water for the first rinse. Put the onion and fat into the bottom of a large saucepan and *sauté* gently for three minutes. Then add the spinach, sugar, seasonings and tarragon, but no water. Cover tightly and steam until cooked; in a pressure cooker this takes less than one minute. *Purée* in a blender. Add enough cream and milk to make a consistency as thick as cream. The flavour is improved if it is left to stand for a few hours before it is served, either hot or cold.

# CREAM OF TOMATO SOUP

5 measuring cupsful skinned, chopped
    tomatoes
½ cupful diced onions
½ cupful chopped carrots
3 tablespoonsful margarine or butter
Salt and pepper
1 dessertspoonful honey or brown sugar
3 dessertspoonsful lemon juice
½ pt. (275ml) cream
1½ tablespoonsful cornflour

Melt the fat and *sauté* the onions and
carrot in it for 3 minutes, then add the
tomatoes, salt and pepper. Simmer for 15
minutes, then *purée* the mixture. Add the
sweetening and lemon juice and let the
soup cook gently for 5 minutes. Mix the
cornflour with the cream, and add to the
boiling soup, whisking all the time. Serve
hot or cold.

# CLEAR MUSHROOM SOUP

½ lb (225g) mushrooms
1½ oz. (40g) nutter or oil
1 small onion
½ stick of celery
¼ lb (100g) french beans
1 teaspoonful of yeast extract
1½ pt (825ml) stock
Salt
Parsley or chives

Wash the mushrooms but do not peel
them, then cut them in thin slices. Cook
the mushrooms in the fat or oil for 2

minutes. Clean the rest of the vegetables,
cut them into thin slices and cook in a
little salted water until tender. Put the
stock into a saucepan, add the cooked
vegetables, except the mushrooms, bring
to the boil and simmer for about 30
minutes. Then add the mushrooms and
yeast extract and simmer for another 5
minutes. Serve chopped chives on top. A
more substantial soup may be made if two
cooked sliced potatoes are added.

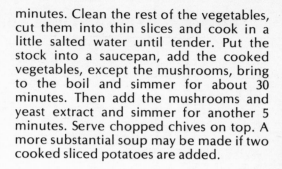

# FRESH ASPARAGUS SOUP

1 lb (450g) fresh asparagus or sprue
1 pt. (550ml) water
1 pt. (550ml) milk
2 oz. (50g) butter
2 oz. (50g) flour
Salt, pepper and dash of nutmeg

Wash the asparagus, cut off the tender tips
and reserve them. Cut the rest of the
asparagus into 1-inch lengths and cook
them in the pint of water for half an hour.
Then throw away the stalks as there is no
further use for them. Cook the tips in the
same water for 5-10 minutes, strain and
keep tips and water. Melt the fat and cook
the flour in it for about 3 minutes, until it
bubbles. Mix the milk with the asparagus
water and add to the *roux* a little at a time
and simmer for about 5 minutes. Add the
asparagus tips and season. Heat up and
serve with chopped parsley or chervil.
Serves from four to six.

## FRESH GREEN PEA SOUP

2 oz. (50g) nutter or butter
⅓ cupful minced spring onions or onion
    tops
2½ lb (1¼kg) peas
Salt and pepper
Dash of nutmeg (optional)
1 heaped teaspoonful sugar
1 teaspoonful fresh chervil
Milk and cream

Melt the fat in a pan and *sauté* the onion in it until tender. Add the peas, seasonings, sugar and nutmeg, the herb and ¼ pt. (150ml) water. Cover and cook until the peas are tender. (In a pressure cooker this will take 1½ minutes.) Add ½ pt. (275ml) milk to the pan and then *purée* the mixture in a blender. Add enough milk or cream and milk to make a soup-like cream. This can be served either hot or cold.

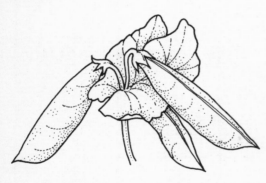

## LETTUCE SOUP WITH ALMONDS

1 medium cabbage lettuce
1 small head of cos lettuce
6 spring onions, minced
2 tablespoonsful nutter or oil
1 teaspoonful turmeric
½ pt. (275ml) milk
½ pt. (275ml) thin cream
½ pt. (275ml) vegetable stock
Salt and pepper
⅓ cupful toasted almonds to garnish

Wash the lettuce and shred it finely. Melt the fat and *sauté* the onion in it for 2 minutes. Mix the onion, lettuce and seasonings, add ⅓ cupful water and steam until tender. (In a pressure cooker it will take about 2 minutes.) Set aside 2 tablespoonsful of this mixture and put the rest through the blender then add the reserved lettuce and turmeric. Thin the *purée* with milk, cream and vegetable stock. Extra cream or stock may be added if liked. Serve hot or icy cold with the toasted almonds.

## MINESTRONE

2 oz. (50g) haricot beans
1 bay leaf
3 oz. (75g) spaghetti
3 carrots
1 small onion
1 stick celery
1 large potato
½ lb (225g) tomatoes or small tin
2 oz. (50g) olive oil
3 oz. (75g) grated cheese
1 qt (1¼l) vegetable stock
Chopped parsley, marjoram, chives and garlic
½ teaspoonful Marmite

Wash the beans and soak them for at least 12 hours, longer if possible. Then cook them in the same water until soft, about 2 hours. Cook the spaghetti in 1 pt. (550ml) of salted water until soft, about 15-20 minutes. Wash, cube and peel the vegetables. Heat the oil in a pan and add the carrots, cook for 2 minutes, then add the celery and onions and then the potatoes. Cook for 10 minutes lifting and stirring the vegetables. Cut up and add the tomatoes then pour in about half the stock and cook gently until all the vegetables are soft. Now add the cooked beans and spaghetti and the water in which they were cooked and the rest of the stock, Marmite and salt, bay leaf and marjoram and finally the chopped garlic. Bring to the boil and simmer for half an hour. Serve with plenty of grated cheese, chopped chives and parsley on each plate.

Cream of Tomato

## MULLIGATAWNEY

2 carrots
2 leeks
1 turnip
$\frac{1}{4}$ lb (100g) celery
1 small apple
2 shallots
1 oz. (25g) white beans
1 qt. (1¼l) stock
3 oz. (75g) butter or nutter
2 teaspoonsful curry powder
1 oz. (25g) sultanas
Large bay leaf
1½ teaspoonsful 81 per cent flour
Lemon juice
Sea salt

Clean all the vegetables and cube them. Peel one shallot and cube it. Melt 1 oz. (25g) of fat in the saucepan and cook the vegetables in it for 8 minutes. Add half the stock and cook the vegetables until they are very tender. Drop in the cooked beans. Heat the rest of the fat in the soup pan, add the other shallot and the apple, both finely chopped, then add the sultanas and cook for 5 minutes.

Mix the flour and curry powder and sprinkle into the pan, stir and cook for a minute or two. Add the salt and bay leaf and cook for 2 minutes then pour in the rest of the stock and cook and stir until the soup is thickened and creamy. All the ingredients should now be blended and the soup cooked for 10 minutes at low heat. Drop in a little lemon juice at the last minute. More curry powder may be added for those who like a more fiery soup.

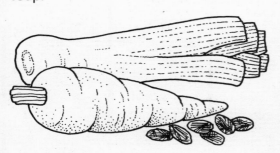

## NOODLE SOUP

2 oz. (50g) noodles
1 qt. (1¼l) vegetable stock
1½ teaspoonsful Marmite
1 oz. (25g) nutter or margarine
Salt
Chopped parsley or chervil

Add the fat to the stock and bring to the boil. Add the noodles and boil until they are soft (about 15-20 minutes). Add the Marmite, salt and parsley to taste.

## POTAGE AUX HARICOTS VERTS

8 oz. (225g) french or runner beans
2 large potatoes
1 small onion or 4 shallots
1 qt. (1¼l) stock
2 oz. (50g) nutter or margarine
2 tablespoonsful cream
2 oz. (50g) 81 per cent flour
½ teaspoonful yeast extract
½ oz. (12g) savoury
Sea salt
Chopped chives

Wash the vegetables, remove the strings from the beans and cut them into diamond-shaped pieces. Peel and cube the onion. Boil the beans and potatoes in the stock until soft. Strain and save the stock. Melt the fat in the soup pan and fry the onion in it until it is lightly browned, add the flour and cook for a couple of minutes then pour in the stock and cook until slightly thickened. Now add the cooked beans and mashed potatoes, the savoury, salt and yeast extract and cook for 10 minutes. Serve sprinkled with chopped chives. Add the cream as it is sent to the table.

Cream of Celery

17

## PURÉED BEET SOUP

8 small beets
1 shallot, chopped
1½ cupsful clear vegetable stock
Pinch ground cloves
Salt and cayenne pepper
1 tablespoonful clear honey
Juice of 1 lemon
Strained orange, grape or grapefruit juice

Scrub the beets and cook them in 1 pt. (550ml) water with the shallot, cook for about 20 minutes. Strain and keep the liquid. Skin the beets and cut them in small pieces then *purée* them in a blender, adding some of the beet water or stock as required. Add the seasonings and thin with stock and beet liquid but do not make too thin. Chill well and serve with blobs of soured cream. Sometimes, leave out the shallot and stock and thin with grape, orange or grapefruit juice.

## PEA AND AVOCADO SOUP

2 oz. (50g) nutter or margarine
⅓ cupful minced spring onions
2 lb (900g) peas
Salt and pepper
1 heaped teaspoonful sugar
Milk or cream or both
Water
1 avocado

Melt the fat in a pan and *sauté* the onion in it until soft. Peel and mash three-quarters of the avocado and mash the large piece. Put the peas, seasonings, sugar into the pan with the onions. Add ¼ pt. (150ml) water. Cover and cook until the peas are done (it will take only about 1½ minutes in a pressure cooker). Add ½ pt. (275ml) milk to the pan and the mashed avocado and *purée* in the blender then add milk to make the *purée* like thick cream. Cut the rest of the avocado into very thin slices and serve as a garnish. This has a superlative flavour.

## PEPPER AND TOMATO SOUP

2 large red or green peppers or tin pimientos
2 lb (1kg) tomatoes, skinned and chopped
1½ teaspoonful grated onion
Sea salt and pepper
⅓ cupful olive oil
¼ cupful chopped parsley

Roast the raw peppers for 25 minutes, then skin them and remove the fibre and seeds. Cut the peppers into strips and marinate them in olive oil for one hour. Then mix the oil, peppers and tomatoes and *purée* them in the blender. Add the parsley and serve hot or cold. If preferred, this soup may be made from a tin of pimientos and then mixed with tomato *purée*.

Do not shrink away from potatoes entirely; a medium-sized potato has the same number of calories as a large orange and is more nourishing.

## POTATO AND LEEK SOUP

4 medium-sized leeks, minced
4 largish floury potatoes, cooked in their skins
1 large onion, minced
3 tablespoonful nutter or oil
Sea salt and pepper
1¼ pt. (700ml) milk
¼ pt. (150ml) thin cream

Trim and wash the leeks, remembering that if the first rinse is in warm water the grit will disappear more quickly. Mince the leeks with the onion and *sauté* them in the hot oil or fat. Peel and dice the potatoes and add to the leeks, add salt and pepper and cook for 2 minutes. Add 1 cupful of water and cook until tender. Put through the blender with milk added then beat in the rest of the liquid. Serve hot or cold scattered with parsley on each serving.

## RASSOLNIK

5 tablespoonful minced pickled cucumber and dill
2½ cupsful vegetable stock
8 very small beetroots
1 dessertspoonful brown sugar or honey
1 pt. (550ml) sour cream
Salt and cayenne pepper
About 4 inches of cucumber, peeled and sliced
2 hard boiled eggs, sliced
½ oz. (15g) fresh dill, chopped

Put the dill pickles to stand in the stock while the rest of the soup is being made. Cut the beet stems in one inch lengths wash the vegetables carefully. Cook them for 20 minutes in 1 pt. (550ml) water with the pan covered. Then put the beets and liquor through an electric blender. Season with salt and pepper and add the sweetening. Add the pickles and stock and, if it needs it, a little lemon juice or vinegar. Chill and add the rest of the ingredients *very* cold. To serve, put some sour cream in each plate, add the soup and mix just a little then garnish with the cucumber, sliced egg and dill.

## SCOTCH BROTH

2 large carrots
1 swede
2 leeks
3 large onions
3 large potatoes
1 tablespoonful top of the milk
2 pt. (1¼l) stock
3 oz. (75g) margarine or oil
6 teaspoonsful Marmite
2 oz. (50g) pearl barley
Sea salt

Cook the barley in 1 pt. (550ml) of the stock until it is tender, it takes about 1½ hours. Peel the vegetables and cut them up small. Melt the fat in a pan and cook the vegetables in it for 8-10 minutes. Then add 1 pt. (550ml) of stock and cook until the vegetables are tender. Mix all the ingredients together and cook for 10-15 minutes. Add the light cream. This soup is a meal in itself.

## SWEET POTATO SOUP (OR BISQUE)

1 lb (450g) sweet potatoes
2 measuring cupsful stock
2 tablespoonsful honey
Dash of nutmeg
$\frac{1}{4}$ pt. (150ml) thick cream
Sea salt
Garnish with toasted almonds, roast chestnuts
 or walnuts

Boil the potatoes then skin and mash them and mix with the vegetable stock, add honey, nutmeg and cream, taste for seasonings. Put a spoonful of sherry in each plate for a luxurious soup, then add the reheated soup and top with the chosen nuts cut in slices.

## SPRING SOUP

All vegetables cooked first
12 asparagus tips
1 cupful shelled peas
2 oz. (50g) carrots in matchstick pieces
1 large tin sweet corn
6-8 cupsful strong vegetable stock
1 small raw tomato, skinned and seeded then
 chopped

Cook the vegetables separately in as little water as possible and use the water for the stock. Use only a very small tomato so that the flavour may not pervade and add only 2 tablespoonsful of asparagus water because of its strong smell.

## TOMATO SOUP WITH DILL

5 measuring cupsful skinned chopped
 tomatoes
$\frac{1}{2}$ cupful diced onions
3 tablespoonsful nutter
Sea salt and pepper
1 dessertspoonful honey or brown sugar
3 dessertspoonsful lemon juice
Garnish with chopped parsley and soured
 cream

Melt the fat and *sauté* the onions and carrots in it for 3 minutes, then add the tomatoes, salt and pepper, simmer for 15 minutes then *purée* in the blender. Add the sweetening and lemon juice and minced dill. Let the soup cook gently for 5 minutes. Garnish each plate with sour cream and chopped parsley. Use hot or very cold.

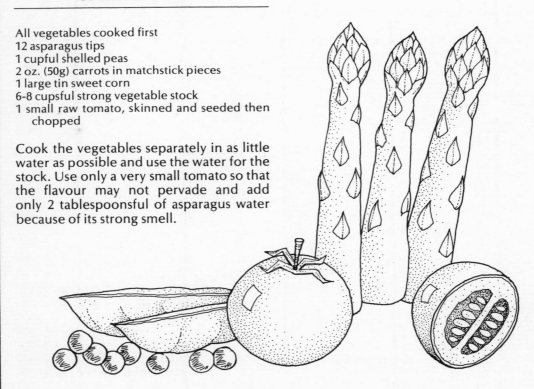

## TOMATO SOUP FROM THE GARDEN

1-1½ lb (450-675g) fresh ripe tomatoes
1 large onion
2 oz. (50g) cooking fat
1 teaspoonful light brown sugar
1 tablespoonful lemon juice
2 pt. (1¼l) stock or
1 pt. (550ml) stock and 1 pt. (550ml) milk or
2pt. (1¼l) milk
1 bayleaf
Salt and pepper

Cut the tomatoes and onion into small pieces. Melt half the fat in a saucepan and cook the tomatoes in it with half the onions until soft. Do not add any water. Rub the tomatoes and onions through a sieve or put through the blender. Melt the rest of the fat, add the rest of the onions and cook until golden then stir in the flour and cook for 4 minutes, stirring. Add the tomatoes and the liquid you have chosen and cook until the flour is slightly coloured. Add the bay leaf, sugar and seasonings. Simmer for about 10 minutes, stirring often. Hand grated cheese with the soup. If this soup starts to curdle, whisk and it should settle down.

## TOMATO AND CELERY SOUP

1 bunch celery
15 oz. (425g) tin tomato *purée* or
Skinned *puréed* fresh tomatoes
2 large onions, sliced
2 carrots, diced
1 teaspoonful Marmite
Sea salt and pepper
2 cloves
½ teaspoonful dried thyme, basil and tarragon
2 dessertspoonsful cornflour
4 tablespoonsful white wine or 1
  tablespoonful vinegar
1 dessertspoonful honey
Garnish with soured cream

Wash the celery and slice it thinly, including some of the freshest green leaves. Put the vegetables (not the tomatoes) in a thick pan with the Marmite, seasonings, cloves, and herbs, use enough stock or water to cover the vegetables. Cover the pan and simmer for an hour and a quarter. When the vegetables are really soft and tender, *purée* them in the electric blender or press through a sieve. Mix the cornflour with a little of the tomato *purée* and add to the soup and check that all the ingredients are in the soup pan. Cook all together for 8-10 minutes. Garnish each serving with a generous spoonful of soured cream on each plate.

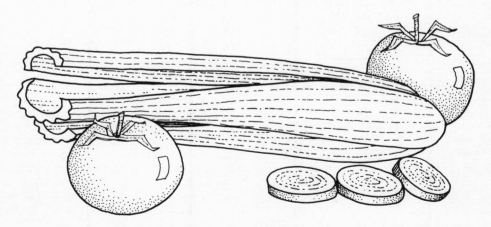

If you have to make soup in a hurry, there is nothing like an electric blender to help you. If cooked vegetables are used it takes only about 5 minutes to prepare the soup.

## QUICK VEGETABLE SOUP

2 tomatoes
¼ small cabbage
1 carrot
Few sprigs of cauliflower
1 oz. (25g) butter or margarine
1 small onion, chopped
½ teaspoonful of Vecon
Sea salt
Chopped parsley or chervil

Wash the vegetables and cut them up and blend them with the stock or water; melt the fat in a saucepan and cook the onion until it is transparent. Add the blended vegetables and cook for 20 minutes. Then add the salt and Vecon. Sprinkle with chopped parsley or chervil.

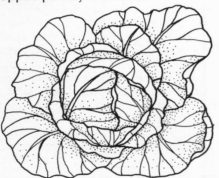

## VEGETABLE MARROW SOUP

2 measuring cupsful peeled, cubed acorn marrow
Good pinch either of ground ginger or mace
2 tablespoonsful honey or brown sugar
Sea salt and pepper
3 cupsful vegetable stock with ½ teaspoonful Marmite
⅔ cupful thin cream
2 tablespoonsful sherry

Cook the marrow until tender, blend until smooth with all the other ingredients. If it is to be served cold, the sherry may go into the blender with the rest of the vegetables, if it is to be served hot, add the sherry last.

## VICHYSSOISE

4 large floury potatoes
1 large onion
3 tablespoonsful butter or nutter
6 large leaks
Dash of nutmeg
Sea salt and pepper
½ pt. (275ml) rich milk
½ pt. (275ml) thin cream
4 measuring cupsful stock with ½ teaspoonful Marmite

Peel the potatoes and onions and dice them finely, put them in a thick pan with the fat and let them cook gently while the leeks are prepared. Trim the leeks leaving on as much of the green as possible, split them and wash carefully, then cut in half-inch lengths, add them and the seasonings and ½ cupful water to the potatoes and onions. Cover the pan tightly and simmer until tender. *Purée* in a blender or sieve them, then mix with the stock, milk and cream. This soup is generally served cold with a garnish of chives. Do not serve it too thick; it may be thinned with milk or cream.

# Chapter Two
# EGG CUISINE

## EGGS À LA GRUYÈRE

4 eggs (free-range)
4 oz. (100g) Gruyère cheese
¼ pt. (150ml) vegetable stock
A nut of vegetable margarine
A little finely-minced parsley and chives
Grated nutmeg and sea salt

Melt the cheese with the margarine, but do this quickly so that the cheese does not have a chance to get stringy as it will if it is overheated. When melted, add the stock and seasoning and mix well. Beat the eggs and beat the herbs into them, then add to the cheese and stir well. Serve with snippets of wholemeal toast.

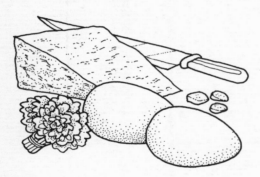

An inexpensive omelette may be made using breadcrumbs. It is suitable for breakfast or for an invalid on a light diet. Older people often find it easier to digest and less rich than more conventional ones.

## BREADCRUMB OMELETTE

4 eggs, separated
½ British standard measuring cupful milk
1 tablespoonful vegetable cooking fat
Salt and pepper
1 cupful breadcrumbs
Beat the egg yolks slightly then add the pepper to them, add the breadcrumbs and milk. Add a little salt to the egg white

and beat until stiff but not dry. Fold into the yolk mixture. Heat the fat in an omelette pan but do not make it too hot because it tends to toughen the eggs. Pour the omelette mixture into the pan and tilt the pan to level it. Put a lid on the pan and cook over low heat so that the bottom is lightly browned: it should take 15 minutes at the right heat. Cook for about 20 minutes altogether until the surface is just dry to the touch. Fold in the usual way and serve with either mushroom sauce or tomatoes in a sauce or grilled.

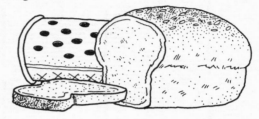

## CARROT BAKE

¼ cupful vegetable fat
3 eggs, separated
Sea salt and pepper
2 cupsful mashed cooked carrots (about 8 carrots)
½ teaspoonful onion salt or grated onion
3 tablespoonsful 81 per cent flour

Melt the fat, add the flour and cook until the flour is golden brown. Leave to cool for a second, add the pepper and onion (or onion salt), the slightly beaten egg yolks and the mashed carrots and mix well. Add a little salt to the egg whites and beat them until stiff but not dry, then fold them into the first mixture or fold the mixture into the egg whites. Line a greased tin with greaseproof paper and pour the mixture into it; set it in a tin of hot water and bake for 30 minutes at 350°F (175°C Gas Mark 4). Leave to stand for 5 minutes after it is done then turn on to a hot dish. Remove the paper and serve in slices with creamed potatoes or a green salad.

# CARROT AND ORANGE SOUFFLÉ

4 eggs, separated
3 tablespoonsful 81 per cent flour
3 tablespoonsful vegetable fat or oil
½ pt. (275ml) milk
Sea salt and pepper
1 heaped tablespoonful minced raw onion
2 large raw carrots, grated
1 heaped teaspoonful grated orange

Make a sauce from the flour, fat or oil and the milk. It is easier to make a smooth sauce if the milk is hot. Add a little salt to the egg whites and whip until stiff but not dry. Add the rest of the ingredients to the egg yolks and beat slightly then pour the sauce over the mixture slowly, stirring all the time. Taste for seasonings and then put into a lightly-greased casserole. Set the casserole in a tin of hot water and bake at 350°F (175°C/Gas Mark 4) for 50 minutes. It has been said that people who swear a carrot shall never pass their lips, have been heard to own that this is a delicious *soufflé*!

## EGG AND CHEESE TIMBALES

½ lb (225g) cheese
3 beaten eggs
2 tablespoonsful cooking fat or nutter
1 tablespoonful 81 per cent flour
1½ cupsful milk
Salt
1½ teaspoonsful spiced fruit sauce
1½ teaspoonsful chopped pimiento

Make a sauce from the flour, fat and milk and stir until thickened. Add the cheese and stir until it is melted. Remove from the heat, add the seasonings and pimiento and pour slowly onto the beaten eggs, stirring all the time. Divide between small moulds or cups, well greased. Put the moulds or cups in a tin of hot water and bake for 45 minutes at 350°F (175°C/Gas Mark 4). Try if they are done before that time is up by sticking a knife in one of them; if it comes out clean, they are ready to eat. Turn out to serve.

## CHEESE AND EGG CAKES

4 beaten eggs
1 tablespoonful grated onion or a little garlic
1 tablespoonful flour
½ teaspoonful salt
Good pinch of paprika
⅓ cupful grated Gouda cheese
Fat or oil for frying

Mix the eggs, onion (or garlic), flour, salt and paprika. Either grate the cheese or cut it in tiny cubes. Heat the fat or oil until a drop of water makes it sizzle. Take a large spoonful of the egg mixture and drop it into the fat. Brown on both sides, turning only once. Serve at once. Strange as it may seem, orange marmalade goes very well with these little crispies.

## PARSLEY AND EGG FRITTERS

4 hard-boiled eggs
1 raw egg
Fried parsley
4 slices fried bread
Breadcrumbs
Seasonings

Slice the eggs and brush them with the beaten raw egg, roll in breadcrumbs and fry in very hot fat. Drain and serve on rounds of crisp fried bread or on toast garnished with the fried parsley. Delicious for breakfast or for a snack later in the day.

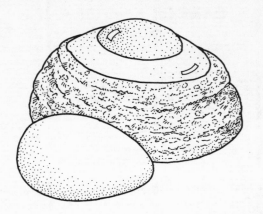

## EGG AND TOMATO CAKE

3 tablespoonsful grated Gouda cheese
4 eggs
1½ lb (675g) tomatoes
1 clove garlic
A little mint and parsley
Salt and paprika
4 tablespoonsful olive oil

Skin the tomatoes and chop the flesh, put them in a pan with the garlic, mint and parsley, add the oil and simmer until the tomatoes are soft. Put in an electric blender or sieve the mixture. Beat the eggs lightly and add the cheese to them and then cook gently in the oil until set. Serve at once.

## EGG NESTS

4 eggs
1 oz. (25g) grated cheese, or
1 oz. (25g) oatmeal biscuit crumbs
Salt and pepper
1 lb (450g) mashed potato

Put the mashed potato in a greased dish and form it into four 'nests', each one large enough to take an egg. Break the eggs, one at a time, into the nests, sprinkle with salt and pepper and cover with crumbs or cheese and bake in the oven at 350°F (175°C/Gas Mark 4) until the eggs are set, about 25-30 minutes.

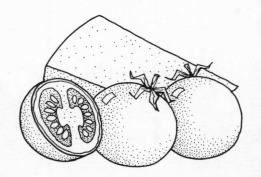

There is something very attractive about a *soufflé* omelette and it is not difficult to make. All it needs is that those who are to eat it must be ready when the omelette is ready – it will not wait for them.

## SOUFFLÉ OMELETTE

2 eggs
2 tablespoonsful hot water
Seasonings
¼ oz. (6g) nutter or margarine

Separate the yolks and whites of eggs whisk the whites stiffly and beat the yolks well. Add the seasonings and hot water to the egg yolks, beat again and then fold into the egg whites. Melt the oil or fat and see that it covers the base of the pan completely. Pour in the egg mixture and cook over moderate heat until the underpart is lightly and delicately brown. Slip under the grill to brow the top and serve as soon as it is dry. Make a slash in the middle, fold it over and slip on to a hot dish. Serve without delay. Four eggs may be cooked at once but do not try more.

Many variations may be made on this basic recipe, so let your imagination lead you to either sweet or savoury omelettes. Never try to put too heavy a filling in a *soufflé* omelette; it is so delicate and cannot bear the strain.

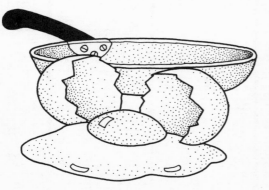

## EGGS WITH POLENTA

8 poached eggs
8 cupsful of polenta meal
¾ cupful Gruyère cheese
¼ cupful grated Parmesan cheese
4 oz. (100g) nutter or margarine
Cayenne pepper
Sea salt
1 pt. (550ml) sour cream

Polenta is coarse-ground yellow corn (maize) meal and is made up this way: for 1 lb (450g) of corn meal you will need 1 teaspoonful of sea salt and 2 qt. (2½l) of water. Boil the water in a thick pan with the salt added. When it is boiling furiously, pour in a slow stream of the corn meal. When half the meal has been added, stir with a wooden spoon and cook for 4 minutes.

If the polenta appears to be getting too thick add more boiling water from a kettle. Continue to cook and stir for about 30 minutes, adding the rest of the meal gradually.

Sprinkle a tea towel lightly with water and spread on a clean surface. Pour the polenta on to the towel and smooth out to about 1½ inches in thickness using a damp knife or spatula. Leave to set for 5 minutes. The Italian method is then to cut the polenta into strips with a cheese wire or a strong thread.

Having made the polenta and allowed it to cool, grease a deep baking dish and place a layer of cheese in the bottom. Dot with nutter or margarine and cover with a ½-inch layer of polenta, then a layer of cheese, and so on, finishing off with a layer of polenta.

Dot with fat and put into an oven pre-heated to 325°F (173°C/Gas Mark 3) and cook just enough to heat through.

In the meantime, poach the eggs. When the polenta is hot make depressions in it and place a poached egg in each one. Serve the sour cream separately.

## EGGS À L'ARDENNAISE

4 eggs
3 tablespoonful thin cream
½ teaspoonful mixed dried herbs
Salt and cayenne pepper

Separate the eggs. Whip the whites until very stiff, beat in the salt, pepper and mixed herbs. Pile the egg whites in a shallow ovenware dish and pour the cream over them. Make slight hollows and drop the egg yolks in one at a time, not touching each other. Bake at 350°F (175°C/Gas Mark 4) until the egg yolks are set. Serve at once from the dish.

## EGGS WITH PORT WINE

6 eggs
2 oz. (50g) margarine
2 teaspoonful finely-chopped shallots
1 tablespoonful 81 per cent flour
1 glass of Port
Pinch of mixed herbs
Sea salt and pepper

Boil the eggs until just hard then cut them in halves lengthwise and keep them warm (the top of a double saucepan is good for this). Make the sauce by melting the margarine then add the shallots, cook for a minute, and stir in the flour until smooth. Mix the port, salt, pepper and herbs and bring to the boil, stirring all the time. Put the eggs on a warm dish and pour the sauce over them and serve at once.

## PUMPKIN OMELETTE

4 eggs
About ½ lb (225g) pumpkin
Margarine
Sugar
Salt and pepper to taste

Peel the pumpkin and cut into very thin slices. Cook gently in a very little salted water, with a little sugar added. Mash when tender and leave to cool, then break the eggs into the *purée*, season and beat well. Heat the fat in a frying pan, pour in the omelette mixture and cook over high heat, lifting the mixture from time to time so that it does not burn. Slide the omelette on to a hot plate, roll it and garnish with parsley.

## ASPARAGUS OMELETTE

⅔ measuring cupful thin cream
2 teaspoonsful cornflour
Dash of nutmeg
Salt and cayenne pepper
5-6 eggs
Salt and pepper
3 tablespoonsful vegetable cooking oil
8-10 cooked asparagus tips
Grated Parmesan cheese

Blend the cornflour and cream and put into a saucepan. Heat and stir in the seasonings and cheese to taste and cook until thickened. This is the sauce. Beat the eggs, cream salt and pepper. Melt the fat in an omelette pan, then cook the egg mixture until set, pushing back the edges so that it cooks evenly. Keep the sauce hot and add the asparagus tips to it; put half the sauce on the cooked omelette, fold it once and slip on to a hot dish. Pour the rest of the sauce on top and sprinkle with a little more of the cheese.

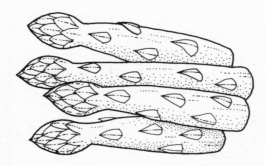

Mix the beaten eggs, broccoli, parsley, salt and pepper, grated onion and cream. Melt the margarine or heat the oil in the omelette pan and pour the egg mixture into it. Cook in the usual way lifting the edges so that all is evenly cooked. When done, but still moist on top, fold over once and slip onto a heated dish. Pour a little olive oil on top and sprinkle well with cheese.

## SWEET CORN OMELETTE

2 tablespoonsful minced celery
3 minced spring onions
2 tablespoonsful butter, nutter or olive oil
6 oz. (175g) cooked sweet corn
4 tablespoonsful hot cream
Salt and cayenne pepper
Chopped parsley or chervil
1 x 4 egg omelette

Melt the butter or heat the oil and *sauté* the onion and celery in it to soften them. Mix the corn and hot cream, add the celery and onion and season with salt and pepper. This is enough filling for a 4-6 egg omelette. Fill the cooked omelette and serve at once garnished with the chopped herb.

## BROCCOLI OMELETTE

1 measuring cupful cooked broccoli
6 beaten eggs
1 tablespoonful chopped parsley
2 tablespoonsful grated onion
¼ cupful cream
3 tablespoonsful oil or margarine
Salt and pepper
Top with olive oil and grated Parmesan cheese

# POTATO OMELETTE

1 measuring cupful fried mashed potatoes
6 eggs
2 tablespoonsful cream
3 tablespoonsful nutter and 1 tablespoonful oil
Salt and pepper
Chopped chives as garnish

Make the omelette by beating the eggs, cream, salt and pepper. Fry it in the mixed hot nutter and oil. See that the potatoes are highly seasoned. Spread onto the cooked omelette, fold once and slip on to a hot dish. Sprinkle the chives on top.

# SPANISH OMELETTE

$\frac{1}{4}$ cupful minced onion
1 diced small green pepper
3 large diced mushrooms
2 tablespoonsful olive oil
3 sliced black olives
1 dessertspoonful lemon juice
2 tomatoes, peeled, seeded and chopped
Salt and pepper
4-6 egg omelette

*Sauté* the green pepper, onion and mushrooms in the oil until tender; add the rest of the ingredients for the sauce and simmer for 5 minutes. Make the omelette as usual; when set but not dry, slip on to a dish but do not fold. Cover with the sauce and chopped parsley.

# Chapter Three
# SUPPER OR MAIN DISHES

## VEGETARIAN PASTRY (1)

4 oz. (100g) wholemeal flour
4 oz. (100g) 81 per cent flour
4-6 oz. (100-175g) margarine, or,
3 oz. (75g) margarine and 3 oz. (75g) vegetable
   cooking fat
Water
Pinch of salt

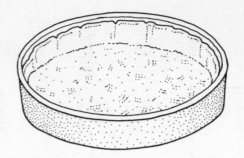

## VEGETARIAN PASTRY (2)

4 oz. (100g) wholemeal flour
4 oz. (100g) rolled oats
4 oz. (100g) margarine
1 egg
4 oz. (100g) wholemeal flour
4 oz. (100g) flaked millet
4 oz. (100g) margarine
1 egg

## BASIC PASTRY FOR SWEET TARTS OR FLANS

Mix Melo crisps with margarine and press into sides and bottom of tin. A little brown sugar may be added.

   Although not strictly pastry, this lining is good but do not fill it until just before it is to be used, because the filling may make it soft and crispness is the great feature of the lining.

## BASIC FILLING FOR FLANS OR QUICHES

4 egg yolks, raw
1 measuring cupful cream
Pepper
Salt
Dash of nutmeg

Mix and add other food to taste, such as 2 medium-sized onions cut in rings and softened in nutter; margarine or oil; or, $\frac{1}{2}$ lb (225g) mushrooms, cut up and *sautéed*; or, pieces of lightly cooked leeks, tomatoes or celery – the list is almost endless.

   All the pastries are made by rubbing the fat into the dry ingredients, then moistening it with water or egg. Line a flan ring with it, put in the chosen filling and pour the egg mixture on top. Slices of Gouda cheese may be used on the base or added to the other ingredients. Bake at 375°F (190°C/Gas Mark 6) until the filling is set and brown on top, about 30-35 minutes. Serve hot or cold.

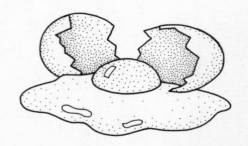

## ARTICHOKES À LA ROMA

8 globe artichokes
1 measuring cupful chopped parsley
$\frac{1}{4}$ cupful chopped pennyroyal (obtainable from a chemist)
$\frac{3}{4}$ cupful olive oil
1 teaspoonful salt
$\frac{1}{2}$ teaspoonful white pepper
2 lemons

Put some cold water and the juice of a lemon in a bowl. Clean the artichokes, remove the tough outer leaves, shorten the others and put them into the water. While the artichokes are soaking, make the stuffing. Mix the parsley, pennyroyal, salt and pepper and some garlic if preferred. Mix well. Take the artichokes out of the water one at a time and pinch the stalks so that the leaves open out a little then push into the spaces as much stuffing as you can.

When all are stuffed, put them in a casserole or deep dish and pour oil into the tops of the artichokes – any left-over stuffing may be sprinkled on top. Add a little water to the casserole, cover very tightly and bake for about an hour at 350°F (175°C/Gas Mark 4). Baste once or twice with the liquor from the dish. Always serve before it gets cool.

## GLOBE ARTICHOKES VINAIGRETTE

1 globe artichoke per person
Boiling salted water
White wine
Olive oil
Salt and pepper
Lemon juice or vinegar
Capers
French mustard

Wash the artichokes and remove the discoloured leaves. Plunge into boiling salted water and simmer for 5 minutes. Lift out of the water and drain upside down. On the basis of six artichokes, put $\frac{1}{3}$ measuring cupful of white wine and the same amount of olive oil in the bottom of a thick saucepan and stand the artichokes in the pan, right side up and close together. Sprinkle a very little salt and pepper on them, separate the leaves a little and put 2 tablespoonsful of olive oil and the same amount of wine in each one. Cover tightly and cook gently for 25-30 minutes, according to size. Mix the juice of one lemon with 2 tablespoonsful of the mustard with a little wine and oil; put in a bowl and serve separately so that each leaf may be dipped into it.

## ARTICHOKES WITH MUSHROOM SAUCE

12 or more artichokes
$\frac{1}{4}$ cupful vegetable stock
$\frac{1}{4}$ cupful white wine
Salt and pepper
$\frac{3}{4}$ cupful sliced mushrooms
2 teaspoonsful 81 per cent flour
$\frac{1}{2}$ cupful cream
Dash of nutmeg

When using whole artichokes, remove the leaves and choke from the vegetables. Cut a thin slice from each stem and peel them. If the hearts are very small use 2-3 for each serving. Roll them in fat over low heat in a large thick pan, add the stock and wine and a little salt and pepper. Cover and simmer for 18-20 minutes until just tender, do not overcook. Test after 15 minutes. *Sauté* the mushrooms in a little fat and when the hearts are cooked, add the mushrooms. Blend the flour with a little cold milk or cream, add the nutmeg and pour over the vegetables and cook until the sauce is thickened. Serve at once. Cornflour is really best for the thickening – it works faster.

Basic Quiche With Mushrooms
Basic Pie

# ARTICHOKES À LA GRECQUE

6 large globe artichokes
1 lemon
1 finely-chopped onion
2 crushed garlic cloves
3 stalks minced celery
1 cupful finely-chopped parsley
½ cupful finely-chopped dill
1 teaspoonful finely-chopped mint
Salt and pepper
⅛ pt. (75ml) olive oil

Wash the artichokes well and with a knife or scissors cut half an inch off the tops of the top leaves and cut the stems level with the bottom leaves. Sprinkle with the juice of the lemon. Cook in boiling salted water for 20 minutes. Drain and leave to cool, then remove enough of the centres to scrape out the hairy section or choke. *Sauté* the onion and garlic in 1 tablespoonful of the oil until soft, then add the celery, parsley, dill, mint, salt and pepper and mix with the oil in a bowl. Stuff the artichokes with this and stand them close together in a large saucepan with oil and water nearly covering them. Cook over low heat for half an hour. Serve either piping hot or chilled.

Not everyone likes the smoky taste of Jerusalem artichokes but they are useful vegetables and can be prepared in different ways. Cheese blends well with the flavour and this is how to make a simple but excellent dish.

# JERUSALEM ARTICHOKES AU GRATIN

1½ lb (675g) artichokes
2 teaspoonsful cornflour
Salt
½ pt. (275ml) thin cream or top of the milk
1 tablespoonful nutter
Dash of nutmeg
½ cupful grated cheese

Wash the artichokes and put them in a pan with ½ pt. (275ml) water; depending on size, they should be tender in 20 minutes. In a pressure cooker they will take only 5 minutes. Keep 3 tablespoonsful of the liquor. Rub off the skins and put the vegetables in slightly salted cold water or vinegar and water or they will turn black. Blend the cornflour and cream, add the artichoke water, the nutter and seasonings and cook until thickened. Mix the sauce with the drained vegetables and put into a shallow baking dish, cover with cheese then put under the grill to melt the cheese and colour it a little.

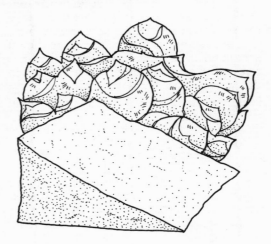

# JERUSALEM ARTICHOKE PANCAKES

1 lb (450g) Jerusalem artichokes
1 small grated onion
1 large beaten egg
¼ cupful 81 per cent flour
Salt
Oil for frying
Pancake batter

Peel the raw artichokes and grate them; drain off some of the juice and mix quickly with the rest of the ingredients, except the oil. Proceed as for other pancakes and serve very hot.

## ASPARAGUS PEAS AND BEET GREENS

2 lb (about 1kg) beet greens or spinach, well
  washed
3 hard-boiled eggs
1 lb (450g) asparagus peas
1 oz. (25g) nutter or margarine
Dash of pepper
½ teaspoonful salt

Boil the spinach and the peas in separate
pans. Do not take the pods off the peas.
Chop the spinach finely and reheat it in
the margarine or nutter in a pan; season it
with salt and pepper. Separate the yolks
from the whites of egg, chop or blend the
egg yolks and mix with the spinach. Make
a mound of spinach and egg on a hot dish
and cover with the drained asparagus
peas; force the egg whites through a ricer
all over the top like a snow cap. Small,
crisp croutons of fried wholemeal bread
look attractive set round this dish.

## HUNGARIAN ASPARAGUS

2½ lb (1¼kg) cooked asparagus
½ pt. (275ml) soured cream
Salt and pepper
2 tablespoonsful lemon juice
½ cupful fresh breadcrumbs
3 tablespoonsful oil or nutter

See that the asparagus is well drained,
then arrange it in a shallow fireproof dish.
Mix the soured cream, salt and pepper
with the lemon juice, heat slightly and
pour over the asparagus. Brown the
crumbs in the nutter or oil and sprinkle
them over the top of the cream. Bake at
400°F (204°C/Gas Mark 7) for not more
than 4 minutes.

## ASPARAGUS AMANDINE

2½ lb (1¼kg) cooked asparagus
¼ cupful melted best margarine or oil
½ cupful soured cream
Salt and pepper
1 tablespoonful grated milk onion
⅔ cupful browned chopped almonds

Put the cooked asparagus in a shallow
baking dish. Mix the fat, soured cream,
seasonings and onion and pour over the
asparagus. Sprinkle the almonds on top
and grill until the top is browned.

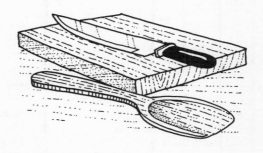

## ITALIAN ASPARAGUS

2½ lb (1¼kg) asparagus
⅓ cupful olive oil
2 cloves crushed garlic
Salt and pepper
1 tablespoonful lemon juice
Grated Parmesan cheese

Cook the asparagus and drain it well, then
serve it in a flat dish. Heat the garlic in the
olive oil and season with salt and pepper
then add the lemon juice. Pour over the
asparagus and sprinkle the cheese on top,
but not too much.

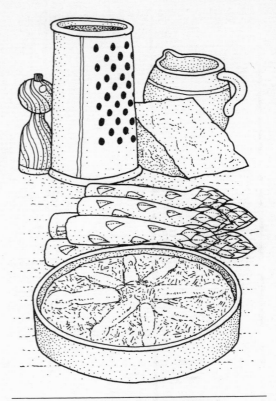

## ASPARAGUS PIE

1 cooked pastry shell
2½ lb (1¼kg) asparagus
2 tablespoonsful cornflour
1½ cupsful thin cream
½ cupful asparagus water
Salt and pepper
2 egg yolks
2 tablespoonsful Parmesan cheese
Garnish of grated cheese

Make a pastry flan case. Cut the tips from
the asparagus leaving them 4 inches long.
Cook until tender in ¾ cupful salted water.
Mix the cornflour with the cream and the
seasonings. Put in a pan and cook and stir
until it thickens, then add the egg yolks
and cheese and cook at low heat only until
the cheese melts. If·preferred, the cheese
may be added and melted and then the
egg yolks quickly stirred in. Arrange half
the asparagus in the baked pastry shell like
the spokes of a wheel, then add half the
sauce; put the rest of the tips on top and
cover with the rest of the sauce. Sprinkle
with Parmesan cheese and put under the
grill to brown the top.

## ASPARAGUS PEAS DELICIOUS

½ lb (225g) asparagus peas
3 tablespoonsful spring onions
2 dessertspoonsful butter or nutter
½ teaspoonful basil
½ teaspoonful clear honey
⅓ cupful water
Salt and pepper

*Sauté* the onions in the butter for not
more than one minute (if preferred, the
onions may be left out and extra peas
used). Take the tips off the pea pods but
do not shell them. Add the peas to the
onions, cover and cook for 5 minutes over
very low heat. Then add the basil, honey,
salt, pepper and water, cover the pan and
cook gently for 5 minutes. They may be
served with a delicate white sauce or just
as they are.

# AUBERGINE WITH YOGURT À LA TURQUE

1½ lb (675g) long aubergines
1 pt. (550ml) yogurt
3 cloves garlic
½ cupful 81 per cent flour
Sea salt and pepper
Oil for frying

Do not skin the aubergine, just wipe and then cut into half an inch thick slices. Dust with flour and fry 4-5 at a time in the olive oil, which should be about a third of an inch deep. Turn once. Remove from the oil when golden brown on both sides and drain on soft paper, sprinkle with salt and pepper. Keep hot and serve yogurt sauce separately. Make the sauce this way: crush the garlic to a pulp, a small garlic press is a must for a vegetarian. Beat the yogurt and garlic together in a bowl. It is easy to do in the blender but the smell of garlic is difficult to remove from it. This sauce is served cold because yogurt cannot be heated.

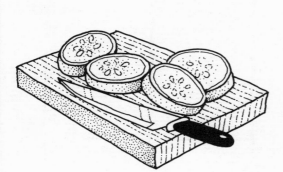

## AUBERGINE CAVIAR

1 medium-sized aubergine
2 crushed garlic cloves
3 tablespoonful olive oil
2 tablespoonful minced young onion tops
Salt and pepper
1 teaspoonful cardamon powder
1 teaspoonful powdered coriander seeds
Black olives and lettuce for garnish

Soak the garlic in the oil. Bake the aubergine whole and unpeeled for 40-60 minutes according to size at 350°F (175°C/Gas Mark 4). Test with a fine skewer or knitting needle. Leave to cool and then peel it and mash the whole of the pulp, then mix in the rest of the ingredients. Serve as a starter garnished with olives on tiny lettuce leaves.

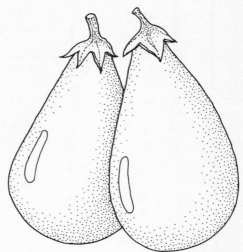

## AUBERGINE BAKED WITH HERBS

1 large aubergine, sliced in half-inch thick slices
Choice of oregano, thyme, tarragon or basil to taste
Salt and pepper

As aubergines absorb a lot of oil as they cook, some people find them too rich and like to season the raw vegetable sliced and then brown them rapidly in a very little oil over high heat. The herb chosen may be sprinkled on the slices at this stage. As the slices brown, put them on a shallow dish or tin and when all the slices are cooked, bake in the oven at 375°F (190°C/Gas Mark 4) for about 20 minutes or until tender. A bran cereal may be scattered on top.

## BAKED WHOLE AUBERGINE

1 very large or 2 smaller aubergines
3 skinned, sliced tomatoes
Basil
Olive oil
Butter or cooking fat
Salt and pepper

Wipe the aubergine and cut a thin slice from each end. Make 4 lengthwise slashes on one side and fill with herbs, salt, pepper and oil. Cover the dish with a tight lid and bake at 350°F (175°C/Gas Mark 4) for half an hour. Then remove the lid, pour in a little more oil in the slits then cover and bake until tender. Test with a knitting needle. Large ones take one hour, smaller ones from $\frac{1}{2}$ to $\frac{3}{4}$ hour. Break open to serve.

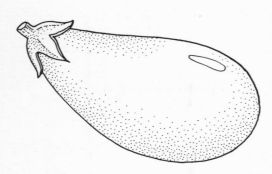

## AUBERGINE PROVENÇALE

2 aubergines
$\frac{1}{2}$ lb (225g) tomatoes
1 small onion
Some chopped parsley
3 tablespoonsful oil
Garlic salt or 1 clove garlic
Salt and cayenne pepper

Trim off the leaves and wipe the aubergine but do not wash it or peel it.

Cut into 1-inch cubes. Cut the tomatoes in halves. Peel the onion and cut it into rings. Heat the oil in a pan and add the garlic or garlic salt and the onion rings; cook for about 6 minutes. Add the tomatoes and aubergine cubes and cook gently until tender. Serve garnished with parsley.

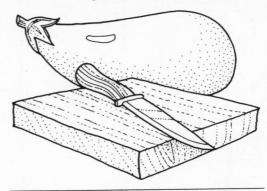

## AUBERGINE PANCAKES

1 large aubergine
2 oz. (50g) 81 per cent flour
$\frac{1}{2}$ teaspoonful baking powder
$\frac{1}{2}$ teaspoonful sea salt
2 tablespoonsful minced young onion tops or chives
Olive or vegetable oil for frying

You need 2 measuring cups full of grated aubergines and for every cupful take 1 tablespoonful of flour. Wipe the aubergines and cut them in pieces and put cut side down in a steamer over boiling water. Cover and cook for at least 10 minutes – skin the aubergine when it is tender. Slice over a bowl and discard any juice, then mash the pulp with a fork but do not liquidize it. Mix all the other ingredients together and then mix with the pulp. If preferred, some of the oil may be mixed with the batter and then there is no need for much oil in the frying pan. Fry on a very hot pan or hot plate until both sides have been browned, then turn down the heat and cook the cakes through. It will take about 3 minutes to get them done. This recipe makes about twelve small pancakes.

## CHINESE AUBERGINES

1 large or two smaller aubergines
4 tablespoonsful sesame or peanut oil
1 dessertspoonful cornflour
1 dessertspoonful light brown sugar
Salt and pepper
1 dessertspoonful soy sauce
1 tablespoonful minced preserved ginger with
  a little syrup
Chopped young onions

Peel the aubergine and cut off the ends which may be tough – a ½-inch slice will do. Slice, brown in the oil then sprinkle with salt and pepper. Place the slices on a shallow baking dish and bake in the oven at 350°F (175°C/Gas Mark 4) until tender (about 15 minutes). Blend the cornflour with 3 tablespoonsful of cold water and put in the top of a double saucepan; add the sugar and soy sauce and cook until thickened. If the sauce gets too thick it may be thinned with a little water or oil. When the aubergine is tender, spoon the sauce over it and sprinkle with ginger and chopped onions. Very small vegetable marrows or courgettes may be cooked this way.

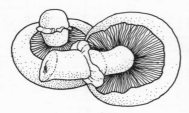

## AUBERGINES AND NOODLE BAKE

6 oz. (175g) shell noodles
1 small aubergine
2 crushed cloves garlic
⅓ cupful olive oil
Salt and pepper
½ cupful tomato sauce
1 teaspoonful dried fennel
¼ cupful breadcrumbs
¼ cupful grated Parmesan cheese

Boil the noodles in salted water for 7-8 minutes, but do not overcook them. Drain off the water. Heat the oil with the garlic in it then mix with the noodles. Peel the aubergine and steam it as above until tender, then add to the noodles. Use some of the best tinned tomato sauce, taste for seasonings and add more if needed, then add the fennel to it. Put the aubergine and noodles in a baking dish and pour on the sauce. Top with crumbs and cheese. Bake at 375°F (180°C/Gas Mark 5) for about 10 minutes.

## CREAMED AUBERGINE

2 aubergines
2 tablespoonsful butter or nutter
⅓ cupful 81 per cent flour
2 tablespoonsful grated cheddar cheese
  (optional)
½ pt. (275ml) thin cream
Salt and pepper
1 teaspoonful marjoram

Bake the aubergines in the oven, whole until tender – the time will naturally depend on the size of the vegetable. While it is cooking, make the sauce. Melt the fat and stir in the flour, cook until it bubbles then cook for a further 10 minutes. Add the cream slowly and when smooth melt the cheese in it, if it is being used. Season with salt, pepper and herb. If the sauce seems too thick do not despair; all will be well because the juice from the aubergines will thin it. Skin the aubergines, mash them, then mix with the sauce and if necessary reheat in the oven. Boiled brown rice may be served with this dish.

## AUBERGINE, TOMATO AND ZUCCHINI CASSEROLE

1 small, sliced aubergine
½ lb (225g) unpeeled zucchini, sliced
1 sliced green pepper
2 teaspoonsful basil
1 teaspoonful tarragon
1 tablespoonful brown sugar
¼ cupful olive oil
2 crushed garlic cloves
2 sliced large onions
Salt and pepper
1½ lb (675g) tomatoes, red and yellow mixed, if possible

Skin and slice the tomatoes and press out a little of the juice or salt them and leave to drain for a few minutes. Then cut them up. Put half the tomatoes in the bottom of a greased casserole and sprinkle with half the herbs, sugar, salt and pepper. Put the olive oil in a pan with the garlic, heat up and *sauté* the aubergine, zucchini, onion and green pepper in it. *Do not cook them all at once. Cook them separately.* Put on top of the tomatoes. Season the vegetables, mix together and bake for 35-40 minutes at 375°F (190°C/Gas Mark 4) for half the time then lower the heat to 350°F (170°C/Gas Mark 4) and cook for the rest of the time.

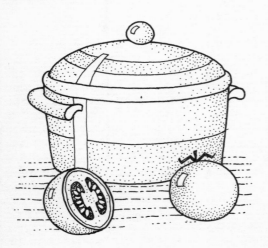

## BROAD BEANS À LA PORTUGAISE

4 measuring cupsful shelled broad beans
1 small onion, finely chopped
2 minced cloves garlic
½ cupful olive oil
A few chopped celery leaves
1 tablespoonsful chopped chervil, dill or a bay leaf
Pepper and salt

Heat the oil and soften the onion and garlic in it; add the beans, celery leaves and the rest of the ingredients. Just cover the ingredients with boiling salted water (be mean with the water) and cook very slowly for 30 minutes. This is a good dish served with crispy noodles. Put noodles in boiling salted water and cook until they are soft: this will not take many minutes. When they are soft, drain them and leave to cool then fry in deep oil until crisp.

## BUTTERED BROAD BEANS

¼ measuring cupful nutter, butter or margarine
6 sliced spring onions
2 lb (about 1kg) shelled broad beans
½ teaspoonful honey
1 teaspoonful dried basil
Salt and pepper
Chopped chives

Put the chosen fat in a saucepan and *sauté* the onions in it for a few minutes; then add the beans, 3 tablespoonsful of water and the rest of the ingredients except the chives. Cover the pan and steam the beans until they are tender (in a pressure cooker it will take about one minute). There will be little or no liquid so do not strain them, just serve with chives sprinkled on top.

## BROAD BEANS AND
## SWEET CORN

1½ lb (675g) broad beans when shelled and
cooked
1 small green pepper, sliced
⅓ cupful diced onion
¼ cupful olive oil
1 cupful cooked sweet corn
Sea salt and pepper
⅓ cupful cream

*Sauté* the onion and green pepper in
the oil until tender. Mix all vegetables,
seasonings and cream. Heat up and serve.

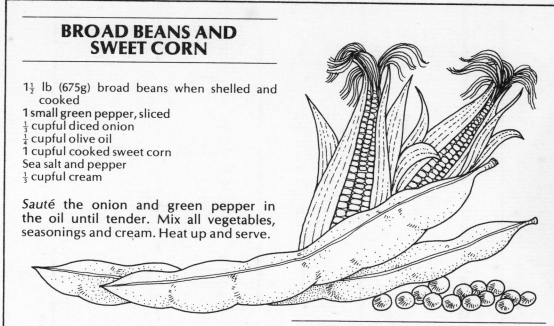

## BROAD BEAN AND
## GREEN PEA CASSEROLE

6 finely chopped spring onions
⅓ cupful margarine
2 lb (about 1kg) broad beans, shelled
2 lb (about 1kg) peas, shelled
Pinch of rosemary
1½ cupsful light cream sauce
¾ cupful grated cheddar cheese
Salt and cayenne pepper

Melt the margarine and *sauté* the onion in
it for one minute (the beans and peas
must be weighed *after* shelling). Add the
beans and peas, ⅓ cupful hot water, the
rosemary, salt and pepper. Cover and
steam until the vegetables are tender.
Make a fairly thick sauce and thin it with
the water from the vegetables. Add ¼
cupful of the cheese to it, taste for
seasonings then mix with the vegetables.
Put all into a greased casserole and
sprinkle the rest of the cheese on top.
Bake in the oven at 350°F (175°C/Gas
Mark 4) to melt the cheese and reheat the
contents.

## BEETROOT IN ORANGE
## SAUCE

2 bunches (approx 680g) small beetroot (the
new crop)
1 tablespoonful vinegar
1 tablespoonful grated orange rind
¾ cupful orange juice
Juice of 1 lemon
1½ tablespoonsful cornflour
Salt and pepper
⅛ teaspoonful powdered cloves
3 teaspoonsful nutter
Chopped chives for garnish

Scrub the baby beets and cook them in 1½
cupsful of water until tender; add the
vinegar to keep them a rich red. When
cooked, strain and keep the liquid, then
skin the beets. Blend the cornflour with
the orange juice, rind, pepper and lemon
juice, add the nutter in a saucepan, stir
and cook until thickened. Add ¼ cupful of
strained beet juice, taste, and if too acid
add brown sugar or honey. Heat the beets
in this sauce then turn into a serving dish
and scatter the chives on top. Large beets
may be served this way but they must be
sliced.

41

## BEETS IN POMEGRANATE SAUCE

8 medium-sized beets
½ cupful pomegranate juice
1½ teaspoonsful cornflour or other thickening
　　agent
1 tablespoonful of honey

Boil the beets as in the previous recipe and skin them. Peel a pomegranate and squeeze in a sieve or blender to extract the juice. Mix the juice with the honey and thickening agent. Cook in a small pan until thickened then heat the beets in this sauce.

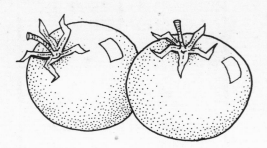

## BEETS IN SOUR CREAM

2 bunches (approx 100g) young beets
2 tablespoonsful oil or margarine
2 tablespoonsful lemon juice
Dash of nutmeg
2 tablespoonsful brown sugar or 1
　　tablespoonful of honey
2 tablespoonsful fresh onion juice (optional)
Salt and pepper
¾ measuring cupful soured cream
Chives or chervil for garnish

Wash the beets and cook them in 1 pt. (550ml) salted water until tender. Strain and keep the liquid and skin and slice the beets. Put the beets in the blender or sieve them, adding some of the juice if needed, then mix in the rest of the ingredients, except the cream. Put the *purée* in a baking dish and cover with the sour cream. Heat for about 8 minutes at 400°F (240°C/Gas Mark 6). Sprinkle with chopped chervil or chives as the dish is being served. This makes an excellent accompaniment to poached eggs.

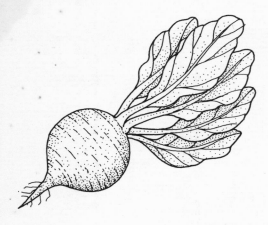

## BEETS IN CRANBERRY SAUCE

2-3 bunches baby beets, boiled
1½ cupsful cranberries
½ cupful orange juice
2 tablespoonsful honey or brown sugar

Skin the cooked beets. Cook the cranberries in the orange juice until soft and then mash them through a sieve or in the electric blender. They must be sieved to remove the skins. Sweeten to taste; heat the beets in the sauce and serve hot. Try serving this with boiled or fried rice or with a plain omelette.

## BEETS BAKED IN SOURED CREAM

12 cooked beets about the size of a tangerine
Salt and pepper
1 dessertspoonful lemon juice
1 dessertspoonful light brown sugar
½ pt. (275ml) soured cream
1½ tablespoonsful margarine or olive oil
Chopped chives or chervil for garnish

Skin and slice or dice the beets. Put all the rest of the ingredients into a saucepan, adding the cream last, then add the beets and heat them. Just reheat the mixture, do not let it even begin to bubble or it will curdle. Send to the table in a serving dish sprinkled with either or both the herbs.

## BEETROOT SOUFFLÉ

2½ cupsful diced cooked beets
1½ tablespoonsful honey
Juice 1 lemon
2 dessertspoonsful fresh onion juice
Dash of powdered cloves
4 large eggs, separated
Salt and cayenne pepper
2 tablespoonsful cornflour
½ cupful fruit juice: orange or grapefruit are best

**Sauce**
Water from the cooking of the beets
Pinch of cloves
Pinch of salt
Honey to taste
1 teaspoonful lemon or grapefruit juice

Wash the beets: you will need 6-8 young ones. Cook the beets in 1 pt. (550ml) water then drain and keep the liquid. Skin and slice the beets then sieve or blend them and mix with the next five ingredients. Mix the egg yolks together and add to the sieved mixture. Blend the cornflour with the fruit juices and add to the beets. All this may be done in a blender. Beat the egg whites to the stiff peak stage and fold them into the beet *purée*.

Grease a 9-inch *soufflé* dish, pour the mixture into it and bake at 350°F (175°C/Gas Mark 4) for half an hour. This *soufflé* should be moist inside. For the sauce, just mix all the ingredients together and serve in a sauce boat. The sauce may be thickened if liked.

## BROCCOLI CASSEROLE

¼ measuring cupful chopped onion
1 sliced green pepper
2 tablespoonsful margarine
2½ lb (1¼kg) broccoli
1½ cupsful thin cream
2 tablespoonsful cornflour or 81 per cent flour
⅔ cupful shredded cheddar cheese
Sea salt and pepper

De-seed the green pepper, slice it and cook the slices in the melted margarine for about 2 minutes. Slice the broccoli and add it with ½ pt. (275ml) water. Cover tightly and cook until just tender. Blend the thickening material with the cream, put in a small saucepan and add the vegetable water; cook and stir until thickened, then season with salt and pepper. Put alternate layers of vegetable and sauce in a casserole, with sauce on top. Cover with the cheese and bake at 425°F (218°C/Gas Mark 7) until the cheese is brown.

## BROCCOLI MOULD

2 lb (about 1kg) fresh broccoli
¼ cupful minced onion
2 tablespoonsful olive or melted margarine
2 tablespoonsful 81 per cent flour
1½ oz. (40g) grated cheese
2 beaten eggs
1½ cupful cooked brown rice (about ½ cupful raw)
1 teaspoonful oregano
Salt and pepper

Any left-over green vegetables or mixture of vegetables may be used for this mould. Cauliflower is good. If potatoes are used, omit the rice. Two cupsful of bread-crumbs may take the place of the rice.

If fresh vegetables are used they should be coarsely chopped, cooked and then strained from the juice, which should be reserved for the sauce.

*Sauté* the onions in the fat for 2-3 minutes then add them to the rest of the vegetables and mix in all the ingredients. Grease a loaf tin and put the mixture into it and bake for half an hour at 350°F (175°C/Gas Mark 4). A delicious sauce may be made by adding ½ cupful of cream to the vegetable liquid, thickening it with flour, then adding a little sherry, grated cheese or *sautéed* mushrooms.

## BRUSSELS SPROUTS WITH CHESTNUTS

1½ lb (675g) small brussels sprouts
15 cooked chestnuts, halved
2 tablespoonsful nutter or oil
2 tablespoonsful fresh onion juice
Vegetable stock
Thickening agent
Dash of nutmeg
Salt and pepper

Wash and trim the sprouts and cook them in ½ cupful salted water, the oil or nutter and the onion juice. Add enough stock to make 1½ cupsful of liquid. Blend the thickening agent with a little stock, add to the sauce and cook until thickened. Season with salt and pepper and a dash of nutmeg. Heat the chestnuts, add to the sauce then blend with the cooked sprouts.

## SWEET AND SOUR CABBAGE

1½ lb (675g) green cabbage, shredded
2 tablespoonsful wine vinegar
2 tablespoonsful nutter
2 tablespoonsful light brown sugar
Black pepper
Sea salt

Melt the nutter in a large pan then add the cabbage, salt and pepper and cover tightly. Cook over very low heat for 25 minutes. Add sugar and vinegar and cook until the cabbage is tender. It must be looked at during the cooking so as to be sure it is not sticking to the pan. Serve very hot. Sliced apples and sultanas may be added. If red cabbage is used, try red wine instead of vinegar. If the pan gets too dry, add a very little water or wine if red cabbage. Try serving crispy noodles with this dish to make a complete meal.

## BAKED CABBAGE WITH GRANNY SMITH APPLES

1 small green cabbage
2 large sour cooking apples
¼ pt. (150ml) unsweetened grapefruit juice
2 tablespoonsful margarine
1 teaspoonful minced chervil
¾ carton soured cream
Salt and pepper

Choose a young fresh cabbage and shred it on a disc shredder. Peel the apples and shred them and mix the two together. Do not add any salt yet because it makes the juice run too freely. Put the mixture into a greased baking diah about eight inches in diameter and pour the grapefruit juice over the vegetable. Cover with a tight lid or cooking foil and bake for half an hour at 350°F (170°C/Gas Mark 4). Heat the margarine, cream and seasonings and pour over the contents of the casserole. Cover again and cook until tender. Season last of all.

## RED CABBAGE WITH CHESTNUTS

1 medium size red cabbage, shredded
1 diced onion
¼ cupful red wine
2 dessertspoonsful honey
½ lb (225g) roasted chestnuts
1 tablespoonful cornflour
½ cupful cream
Dash of nutmeg
Salt and black pepper

Clean the cabbage and shred it. *Sauté* the onion in the margarine for about 1 minute, then add the cabbage, wine and honey. Cover and cook until the vegetable is just tender, but do not overcook. Shell the chestnuts and cut them in halves. Mix the cornflour and cream, add the seasonings and blend with the liquid drained from the cabbage and cook until it thickens a little, then fold lightly into the cabbage. Serve very hot.

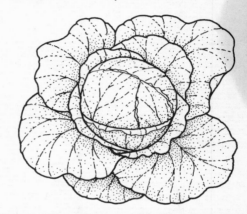

## CHINESE CABBAGE IN CHINESE STYLE

1 Chinese (celery) cabbage
1 crushed clove of garlic
¼ cupful soy or peanut oil
1 tablespoonful ginger root
1 tablespoonful cornflour
1 tablespoonful sherry
1 teaspoonful soy sauce
Minced spring onions as garnish

Wash the cabbage and slice it thinly and reserve the loose leaf ends. Put the solid part of the sliced leaves in a big frying pan with the oil and garlic and cook for 3 minutes over low heat; then add the loose, tender leaves, salt and ginger root. Cover and steam until just tender. Blend the cornflour with 2 tablespoonsful of cold water, add the sherry and soy sauce. Stir into the cabbage and it will thicken. Do not cook the cabbage for more than 3 minutes after this; it must still be crisp.

## DOLMAS

Real dolmas are always rolled in vine leaves, but it is not always possible to buy vine leaves and cabbage leaves are a good substitute.

**Stuffing**
1½ cupsful minced walnuts
¼ cupful minced spring onions
1 cupful cooked brown rice
¼ cupful olive oil
1 beaten egg
Sea salt and black pepper
1 teaspoonful oregano
6 minced mint leaves
½ cupful sultanas
3 tablespoonsful chopped parsley
½ teaspoonful cinnamon
3 teaspoonsful honey
1 teaspoonful thyme
½ cupful pine nuts (pignolias)

Blanch the cabbage leaves in boiling water for from 5-8 minutes, no longer, then drain and cut out the thick ribs from the leaves. Soften the onions in the oil, then mix all the ingredients together. Put some of the stuffing on each leaf and roll up from the stalk ends and tuck the sides in when rolling as though making a parcel.

Put the little rolls close together in a casserole or other covered baking dish and add ¼ pt. (150ml) of seasoned vegetable stock and ¼ cupful olive oil. Cover tightly and cook at 325°F (160°C/Gas Mark 3) for one hour. A sauce may be made from the strained liquor in the baking dish, though it will need to be thickened slightly. Alternatively, serve tomato sauce, sour cream, mushroom or mustard sauce. If dolmas are made very small, they make good 'starters'.

## CARROTS COOKED IN STOCK

1½ lb (675g) very young carrots, washed, not scraped
½ cupful oil, melted nutter or margarine
2 teaspoonsful light brown sugar
1 cupful vegetable stock, white wine or water
Salt and pepper
1 teaspoonful lemon juice

Cook the carrots in a thick pan with a lid. Slice the carrots thinly. Melt the fat or heat the margarine or oil and add the carrots, sprinkle with sugar, salt and pepper, cover tightly and leave to cook over very low heat. Turn the slices over when they begin to brown, then add half the liquid; cover again. Cook until the carrots are tender and nearly dry.

Carrots are among the most valuable vegetables in our garden for they contain more vitamin A than any other vegetable. Many people find the flavour of carrots too bland, but they mix well with other vegetables. Always cook them in the minimum of water and then use the water for soups or for sauces.

## BUTTERED CARROTS WITH HERBS

2 bunches new carrots
1 tablespoonful lemon juice
1 tablespoonful margarine
Salt and cayenne pepper
Choose from the following herbs: minced tarragon, parsley, spring onions, chervil, basil

Trim and wash the carrots and leave whole as long as they are small and tender. Put them in a thick pan with the lemon juice, margarine, 3 tablespoonful of water, salt and pepper. Cover the pan and simmer for 10 minutes. Put the carrots in a hot dish, add more margarine if liked and sprinkle generously with the chosen herb or herbs.

## CARROTS WITH LEMON OR ORANGE SAUCE

1 bunch of young carrots
1 tablespoonful lemon juice
2 tablespoonsful nutter
1 dessertspoonful cornflour
Salt and pepper
$\frac{1}{3}$ cupful orange juice
2 tablespoonsful honey
1 tablespoonful minced parsley

Cook the carrots in the lemon juice, $\frac{1}{2}$ cupful water, salt and pepper and the margarine. Blend the cornflour with the orange juice, sweeten with honey and mix with the liquid in which the carrots were cooked then cook until thickened. Dish the carrots and pour the sauce over them and sprinkle with the parsley. If lemon sauce is wanted, use 3 tablespoonsful of lemon juice instead of the orange juice.

## CARROT RING

$2\frac{1}{2}$ measuring cupsful mashed, cooked carrots
2 dessertspoonsful lemon juice
1 teaspoonful prepared mustard
$4\frac{1}{2}$ teaspoonsful grated onion
$1\frac{1}{2}$ tablespoonsful chopped parsley
1 teaspoonful salt
$\frac{1}{4}$ teaspoonful black pepper
2 tablespoonsful 81 per cent flour
2 tablespoonsful melted margarine or oil
6 oz. (175g) dry breadcrumbs
$\frac{1}{2}$ pt. (275ml) thin cream, scalded
4 eggs, separated

Mix the carrots with the next ten ingredients. Beat the egg yolks and add them. Whip the egg whites to the stiff peak stage and fold them in. Grease and flour a ring mould and put the mixture into it. Set a tin of water in the oven and stand the ring in it. Bake for 30-35 minutes at 350°F (175°C/Gas Mark 4) when the contents of the tin should be set. Take out of the oven and leave to stand for 3 minutes before removing from the tin. The middle may be filled with cooked green peas, stewed tomatoes, or scrambled eggs.

## CARROTS, APPLES AND ORANGES

8 young carrots, shredded
3 large sour apples, shredded
$\frac{1}{4}$ pt. (150ml) orange juice
Grated rind of 1 orange
$\frac{1}{2}$ cupful melted margarine or oil

Mix the apples and carrots and put them in an ovenware dish. Pour the orange juice over them and add the grated rind. Cover the dish and bake for 35-40 minutes at 325°F (160°C/Gas Mark 3). When just tender, season the margarine or oil with salt and pepper and pour over the contents of the dish.

## CARROT AND ORANGE SOUFFLÉ

2 measuring cupsful cooked mashed carrots
2 tablespoonsful honey or light brown sugar
Good dash of mace
$\frac{1}{4}$ cupful orange juice
4 minced spring onions
$\frac{1}{2}$ cupful orange juice
Juice of $\frac{1}{2}$ lemon
3 tablespoonsful cornflour
3 eggs, separated

Cook the carrots with the honey or sugar, the mace, salt and pepper, the *half* cup of orange juice and the onions. Blend the *quarter* cup of orange juice with the lemon juice and the cornflour and stir over low heat until thickened. Put the two mixtures through the blender with the egg yolks. Fold in the stiffly beaten egg whites at the last. Pour into a greased *soufflé* dish and bake at 350°F (175°C/Gas Mark 4) for 25 minutes.

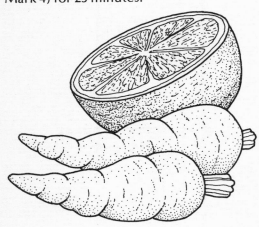

## BRAISED BELGIAN CHICORY

2 heads of chicory
4 tablespoonsful nutter, margarine or oil
$\frac{1}{2}$ cupful water or vegetable stock
Salt and pepper
Grated Parmesan cheese

Clean the chicory and remove any discoloured leaves. Melt the fat in a thick frying pan with a lid. Add the chicory and brown it lightly turning it from time to time. Then add the liquid, cover the pan and cook until the chicory is tender. There should be no liquid left when this is done. Sprinkle with cheese and serve with a plain omelette. (Celery or fennel may be used instead of chicory.)

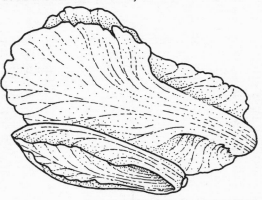

## BRAISED CELERY AND MUSTARD

4 cupsful sliced celery
3 tablespoonsful olive oil
2 tablespoonsful margarine
1 teaspoonful dried fennel
$\frac{1}{3}$ cupful thick cream
1 tablespoonful of french mustard
Salt and pepper

Cut the celery into 1-inch lengths and put it with the olive oil, margarine, salt, pepper and fennel into a strong pan or casserole (if preferred, basil may be used instead of fennel). Put the uncovered casserole into the oven at 400°F (200°C/Gas Mark 6) and cook for 10 minutes, then lower the heat to 350°F (175°C/Gas Mark 4) and cook for 12 minutes longer, then turn into a serving dish. Put the cream and mustard into the casserole and heat it and mix it well, then pour over the celery. If the celery is not very tender and young, extend the cooking times.

## CELERY WITH NUTS AND CREAM

1 medium-sized bunch green celery
Juice ½ lemon
½ pt. (275ml) vegetable stock
Pinch of thyme
1 teaspoonful golden syrup
¼ pt. (150ml) thin cream
⅓ cupful grated cheddar cheese
¼ cupful chopped nuts, either almonds or
    mixed nuts
Salt and pepper

Wash and trim the celery and cut it into 2-inch lengths. Wash again and arrange on the bottom of a shallow ovenware dish. Squeeze the lemon juice over it, add the stock, thyme and syrup. Bake at 325°F (160°C/Gas Mark 3) for 30 minutes. Strain off the liquor and measure ½ cupful of it into a saucepan, then add the seasonings, cream and cheese. As soon as the cheese melts pour it over the celery and scatter the nuts on top.

*Sauté* the leeks in the margarine for 2 minutes, add the celery and ⅓ cupful water, salt, pepper and cover tightly. Cook until the vegetables are tender. Put in an ovenware dish. Measure the juice and add enough cream to make 1½ cupsful of liquid. Blend the cornflour with a little milk or water and add it. Mix and add the curry powder and turmeric and cook until thickened, then pour over the vegetables. Put the cheese on top and brown in a hot oven or under the grill.

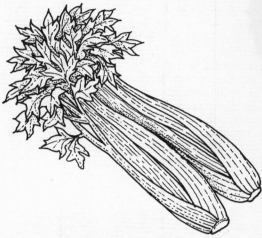

## CREAMED CELERIAC

2 lb (about 1kg) celeriac
¼ cupful diced mild onion
3 tablespoonsful margarine
3 tablespoonsful vegetable stock
½ cupful thin cream
2 teaspoonsful cornflour
Salt and cayenne pepper
Grated cheese

Peel the celeriac and cut it into strips ½ inch long and ½ inch wide. *Sauté* the onion in the fat for a minute or two, add the celeriac and stock. Cover tightly and cook until the celeriac is tender. Blend the cream and cornflour and season with salt and pepper. Cook until it thickens then add the celeriac, etc. Put in a serving dish with cheese on top. The cheese may be omitted.

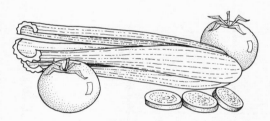

## CREAMED CELERY AU GRATIN

⅔ cupful minced leeks
3 tablespoonsful oil or margarine
3 cupsful sliced celery
Celery liquor plus light cream to make 1¼
    cupsful
2 dessertspoonsful cornflour
1 teaspoonful curry powder
1 teaspoonful turmeric
½ cupful grated cheddar cheese
Salt and pepper

# BUTTERED CHARD

1½ lb (675g) chard
1 mild onion or 6 spring onions
1 small green pepper, chopped
2 tablespoonful olive oil
½ teaspoonful basil
2 teaspoonful lemon juice

Wash the chard then separate the leaves from the ribs, cut the ribs into 2-inch lengths. Heat the oil and *sauté* the onion and green pepper in it; do this in a thick pan. After they have cooked for a minute, add the chard ribs and cook for another minute, then add the leaves, which may be cut or torn if very large. Add salt and pepper, lemon juice and herb. No water is needed as with spinach. Cover the pan and cook over very low heat until the chard is tender (about 15-20 minutes). Serve very hot.

If preferred the chard may be cooked as in the former recipe, since it gives it more flavour. Make a sauce from the fat, flour and chard liquid and cook until thickened. Take off the heat and allow to cool slightly, then beat in the egg yolks. Mix the sauce and chard, etc. Beat the egg whites until very stiff and then fold them into the mixture. Put in a casserole or *soufflé* dish and bake for 40 minutes at 350°F (170°C/Gas Mark 4). The *soufflé* should be a little soft inside.

# CHARD CASSEROLE

1 making of buttered chard
1½ cupsful liquid from the chard plus cream
1½ tablespoonsful cornflour
½ lb (227g) *sautéed* mushrooms
½ cupful minced shallots
½ cupful grated Swiss cheese

Mix the liquid from the chard with the cream and cornflour and cook until thickened. Grease a baking dish or casserole and put in half the chard, cover with mushrooms and onion and then add the rest of the chard. Pour the sauce over all. Cover and cook for 15 minutes at 350°F (170°C/Gas Mark 4). Uncover and sprinkle with cheese and bake for 10 minutes longer. If liked, the cheese may be omitted and oiled breadcrumbs or cornflakes used instead.

# CHARD SOUFFLÉ

1½ measuring cupsful minced or *puréed* chard
2 tablespoonsful oil or margarine
3 level tablespoonsful 81 per cent flour
Drained liquid from the chard and thin cream
    to make 1 cupful
½ teaspoonful dried thyme
3 eggs, separated
Salt and pepper

## EASTERN SHORE CORN PUDDING

2 cupsful tinned, creamed style corn
1 egg yolk, lightly beaten
1 egg white beaten stiff
1 pt. (550ml) milk
2 tablespoonsful melted fat
1 level teaspoonful sea salt
Good pinch cayenne pepper and sugar
$\frac{1}{4}$ grated nutmeg

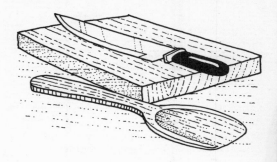

Mix all the ingredients together, folding the egg whites in last. Turn into a greased baking dish and cook at 325°F (160°C/Gas Mark 3) for about half an hour until set. It should have a golden brown top with custard underneath, like a savoury baked custard. Good with a crisp green salad.

## CORN FRITTERS (1)

1 cupful tinned cream style sweet corn
1 cupful 81 per cent flour
1 piece of nutter the size of a walnut, melted
1 egg, separated
$\frac{1}{2}$ teaspoonful baking powder
Cayenne pepper and salt
Cooking fat or oil

Sift together the flour, salt, pepper and baking powder then mix in the corn. Add the melted nutter, egg yolk and milk and mix well. Fold in the stiffly beaten egg white. Have ready a frying pan with about $\frac{3}{8}$ inch of smoking hot fat in it and drop the batter in from a tablespoon. Do not cook more than 2-3 fritters at a time or the fat will get too cool. Turn the fritters once. When golden brown and crisp, dry on soft paper. Keep hot to serve with the sauce and perhaps with a dish made from eggs. The fritters go well with scrambled eggs and try adding a very little horseradish to the eggs.

## CORN FRITTERS (2)

4 oz. (100g) 81 per cent flour
Good pinch of salt
1 dessertspoonful brown sugar
2 eggs, separated
2 tablespoonsful melted margarine or oil
About $\frac{1}{8}$ pt. (75ml) milk
1 large tin corn
Deep fat for frying

Mix the flour and salt. Mix the egg yolks, sugar, margarine or oil and milk to make a thick batter. Stir in the corn. Whip the egg whites until very stiff and then fold into the first mixture. Have a pan of hot oil ready and drop in the fritter batter when the oil is at 375°F (190°C/Gas Mark 5). Cook two or three at a time and keep warm on soft paper in a very cool oven. Serve sauce or not, as you please.

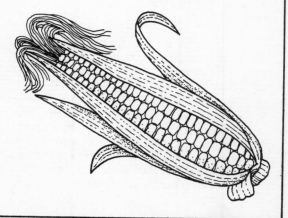

## SAUTÉED CORN

2 large onions, sliced thinly
1 large green pepper, seeded and sliced thinly
2 oz. (50g) best margarine
2 cupsful raw corn kernels
Salt, pepper and paprika

*Sauté* the onions and green pepper in the margarine and, when tender, add the corn and stir gently and cook for 10 minutes. Stir often or it will burn. Season and serve.

## BAKED SWEET CORN AND SPANISH ONIONS

1 onion per person
Dash of powdered cloves
Sea salt and pepper
2¾ cupsful cooked corn (or tinned)
Sauce
4 teaspoonsful cornflour
Onion water plus thin cream to make ¼ pt. (150ml)
1 teaspoonful turmeric
Grated cheese

Cut the peeled onions into very thick slices and steam them until tender in a very little water. They must not become mushy and should be lifted out of the pan before this happens. Lift them into a greased baking dish and season with cloves, salt and pepper, then cover with the corn. Make a white sauce, about ¾ pt. (425ml), in the usual way then pour over the contents of the dish, sprinkle with cheese and reheat in the oven until lightly browned.

## PIMIENTOS FILLED WITH SWEET CORN

1 large tin pimientos
1 large tin corn
Beaten eggs
Melted nutter or margarine
Sea salt and pepper
Parsley

Grease little fancy moulds or small cups into which a whole pimiento will fit. For each cupful of corn allow 2 beaten eggs, a little melted nutter, salt and pepper. Mix well and fill the pimientos with the mixture and put on a tin and bake at 350°F (170°C/Gas Mark 4) for about 15 minutes. Turn out when done and garnish with parsley.

## SWEET CORN BATTER CAKES

2 oz. (50g) 81 per cent flour
1 teaspoonful baking powder
½ teaspoonful sea salt
2 cupsful cooked corn
½ pt. (275ml) milk or a cupful of mixed milk and sour cream
2 eggs, separated

Sift the dry ingredients together and mix in the corn. Add the milk and egg yolks (here a little soya cold be used instead of one of the eggs). Beat the egg whites until stiff and fold into the batter. Heat a hot girdle, griddle or hot plate, even a strong frying pan, and drop the batter on to it from the tip of a spoon (if you want round cakes) from the side of the spoon (if you like oval ones). Fry like drop scones. Makes about eight pancakes.

## SWEET CORN CUSTARD

1 teaspoonful dried onion flakes soaked in a
   little water
1 green pepper, de-seeded and diced
3 tablespoonsful oil, nutter or margarine
3 tablespoonsful uncooked corn
Pinch of nutmeg
1 tablespoonful sugar
$\frac{3}{4}$ pt. (425ml) milk
3 beaten eggs
Salt and pepper

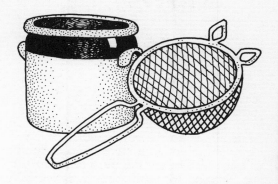

Melt the fat and dry the green pepper and
onion in it until tender, then add them
and the fat to the corn. Season with salt,
pepper and sugar, then stir in the beaten
eggs and the milk. Grease a baking dish
and turn the mixture into it. Bake until set
at 350°F (175°C/Gas Mark 4), about 25
minutes.

## CREAM OF
## CORN DELICIOUS

1 tablespoonful grated onion
3 tablespoonsful minced green or red pepper
3 tablespoonsful nutter or margarine
1 large tin corn
$\frac{1}{2}$ teaspoonful salt
Black pepper
$\frac{1}{2}$ pt. (275ml) thin cream
3 eggs separated

Melt the fat and fry the onion and pepper
in it until soft. Put into a slightly warmed
mixing bowl and add the rest of the
ingredients except the egg whites which
must be beaten to the stiff peak stage and
then folded in. Pour into a greased
ovenware dish and bake at 350°F
(175°C/Gas Mark 4) for 15 minutes.

## CORN SOUFFLÉ

$1\frac{1}{2}$ cupsful sweet corn
1 little red pepper, de-seeded and diced
1 teaspoonful sea salt
1 dessertspoonful 81 per cent flour
2 dessertspoonsful grated cheddar cheese
$\frac{1}{4}$ pt. (150ml) cream
4 egg yolks and 3 egg whites

Mince the corn and pepper in the mincer;
blend the flour, salt and cheese and beat
in the cream. Put these ingredients into a
pan and bring just to boiling point, then
pour over the well-beaten egg yolks. Now
mix in the corn and red pepper and fold
in the stiffly beaten egg whites. Grease
and prepare a *soufflé* dish and pour the
mixture carefully into it. Bake at 350°F
(175°C/Gas Mark 4) for half an hour.
Serve at once. Sauce may be served if
liked.

## SWEET CORN BAKE

12 ears of young sweet corn
½ pt. (275ml) cream
2 tablespoonsful melted nutter
3 eggs, separated
Salt and pepper
Nutmeg (optional)

Grate all the corn from the cobs using the back of a large table knife. Be sure to get all the milk out. Add the cream to the corn, season with salt, pepper and a dash of nutmeg. Stir in the melted nutter and then the egg yolks. Lastly, fold in the stiffly beaten egg whites. Grease a baking dish generously, pour the mixture into it and bake for 35-40 minutes at 300°F (145°C/Gas Mark 2), then raise the heat to 375°F (190°C/Gas Mark 5) and brown the top. This will take about 10 minutes. May be served hot or cold.

## DILL DUMPLINGS WITH TOMATO SAUCE

**Dumplings**
8 oz. (225g) 81 per cent flour
½ teaspoonful salt
1 heaped teaspoonful baking powder
1 teaspoonful margarine
1 teaspoonful cooking fat
3 tablespoonsful fresh dill leaves
¼ pt. (150ml) milk

**Tomato Sauce**
1½ tablespoonsful nutter
3 tablespoonsful sliced onion
2 cupsful tomato juice
Salt and pepper
Garnish of chopped parsley

*Sauté* the onion in the nutter until it is soft, add the tomato juice, salt and pepper and bring to the boil. To make the dumplings, sift the dry ingredients together, put in the nutter and cooking fat, add the dill and mix then add enough milk to make a soft but not sticky dough. Nip off nine pieces and roll into balls. Roll in flour and put in the refrigerator for 12 minutes. Bring the sauce to the boil and, if preferred, thicken it a little then drop in the dumplings and cover and cook for 12 minutes. Sprinkle the cooked dumplings with parsley.

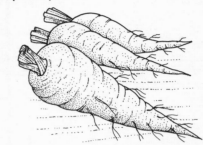

## FRITTATA VERDI

½ cupful chopped cooked spinach
2 tablespoonsful chopped parsley
2 tablespoonsful chopped chervil
4 beaten eggs
1 tablespoonful cream
3 tablespoonsful nutter or olive oil
1 tablespoonful grated Parmesan cheese
1 tablespoonful spinach water
Salt and pepper

Mix the spinach, herbs and seasonings. Use fresh herbs whenever possible. Beat the eggs until light and pale, add the cream and beat again then beat in the spinach water. Add one tablespoonful of cheese and mix lightly with the greens. Melt the nutter (or oil) in a frying pan and cook the egg-spinach mixture over a fairly high heat, lifting the side a little to allow the uncooked part to run underneath. When cooked and set, but not dry, empty into a round serving dish but do not fold it. Put more cheese on top. This will serve two people.

# HOPPITY JOHN

1 pt. (550ml) dried beans (any kind)
1 onion
Salt and pepper
2½ pt. (1½l) cold water or vegetable stock
1 cupful raw rice
1 pt. (550ml) water
2 teaspoonful lemon juice
2 tablespoonsful nutter
Salt

Soak the beans in water for 24 hours then drain off and put the beans in a large thick pan with the onion, salt and pepper and the cold water. Bring to the boil and simmer for 2 hours until they are tender. Lift out the onion and pour off all the water. In another saucepan mix the rice, water, lemon juice, nutter and salt to taste, bring to the boil and stir once with a fork. Cook, uncovered, for 20 minutes until the rice is dry and fluffy. Mix the rice and beans, add a tablespoonful of nutter or margarine and taste for seasonings. Simmer the mixture for 10 minutes.

# KALE WITH CHEESE SAUCE

1½ lb (675g) curly kale
½ cupful minced onion
A little nutter or margarine
Salt and pepper
1 dessertspoonful lemon juice

**Sauce**
1 dessertspoonful nutter or margarine
2 dessertspoonsful 81 per cent flour
¼ pt. (150ml) thin cream
Grated cheese for the top

Wash and remove the stems from the kale and cut the leaves into pieces. *Sauté* the onion in the nutter for 2 minutes, then add the kale, salt, pepper, lemon juice and 2 tablespoonsful of water. Cover tightly and cook until tender.

To make the sauce, melt the fat, stir in the flour and cook over low heat until it bubbles, then blend in the cream and cook until thickened. Add the cheese and drain the liquor from the kale into the sauce and stir until blended. Put the kale and sauce into a greased baking dish and sprinkle thickly with cheese. Then grill to melt and brown the cheese.

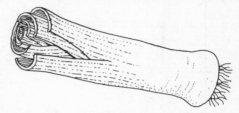

# BRAISED LEEKS IN VEGETABLE STOCK

2 lb (1kg) medium size leeks
2 tablespoonsful nutter or margarine
¼ pt. (150ml) good vegetable stock
2 teaspoonsful cornflour
3 teaspoonsful lemon juice
Salt and pepper
Parsley or chervil for garnish

Trim the roots off the leeks and remove some of the outer leaves, which will be tougher than the inner ones (well washed, these leaves should go into the stock pot). Trim the green part but leave as much as possible. Wash the leeks well – it helps if warm water is used for the first wash with cold used after. Only buy the largest leeks if there is no alternative; if you have large ones, split them down the middle.

Put the leeks into a thick pan, add the nutter, seasonings and stocks. Cover and simmer until the leeks are just tender, about 10-12 minutes according to age, or size. Blend the cornflour and lemon juice and add 1 dessertspoonful cold water, add to the pan and cook until like cream. Lift the leeks and sauce onto a hot serving dish and sprinkle parsley or chervil on top. It is best to serve the leeks on toast because the water clings to them and weakens the sauce.

## LEEKS AND BROWN RICE

6 oz. (175g) raw brown rice
1 pt. (550ml) vegetable stock
3 large or 6 smaller leeks, minced
3 tablespoonful nutter or margarine

Cook the rice in the seasoned stock for 45 minutes. Do this with the pan covered and the heat very low. *Sauté* the minced leeks in the fat, then stir in the rice and leave to stand on the cooker but without heat. Good as a side dish with a plain omelette.

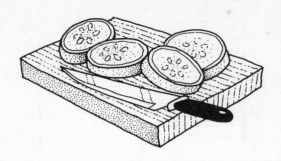

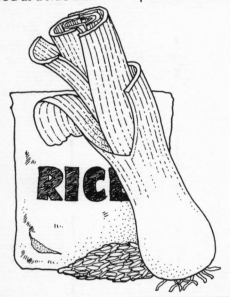

## CREAMED LEEKS

2 lb (about 1kg) leeks
2 tablespoonful nutter
$\frac{1}{8}$ pt. (75ml) vegetable stock or Marmite and water
$\frac{1}{4}$ pt. (150ml) thin cream
2 teaspoonful cornflour
Salt, pepper and paprika

Trim the leeks leaving as much green as possible. Wash them well and if they are large split them in halves. Heat the fat and soften the leeks in it; add the stock. Cover with a tightly fitting lid. Cook gently until just tender. Blend the cornflour with the cream, add salt and pepper and mix with the leeks. When the sauce is thickened and smooth, dish the leeks and sauce and sprinkle lavishly with paprika. Grated cheese may be handed with this dish if liked.

## LEEKS AND NOODLES

6 medium-sized leeks cut in half-inch pieces
3 tablespoonful nutter or margarine
Salt and pepper
$\frac{3}{4}$ lb (325g) shell macaroni or ribbon noodles
Boiling water
Grated cheese

*Sauté* the leeks in the fat then season with salt and pepper. Boil the shells or noodles in plenty of water, lightly salted, for about 7 minutes, or until tender. Drain and send to the table mixed with the leeks and covered with cheese.

## LEEKS WITH LEMON SAUCE

2 lb (1 kg) leeks
3 tablespoonful nutter or margarine
3 tablespoonful lemon juice
$\frac{3}{4}$ teaspoonful cornflour
Salt, pepper and paprika
Slices of crisp buttered toast
Garnish with 2 sliced, hard-boiled eggs

Heat the cleaned, trimmed leeks in the nutter. Add about 2-3 tablespoonsful of water, the lemon juice and seasonings. Cover and cook gently for about 8 minutes or until just tender. Mix the cornflour with a tablespoonful of cold water and stir into the leeks and cook until the sauce thickens. Put the toast in a dish and serve the leeks on the slices. Spoon the sauce over them. Mash the hard-boiled eggs and sprinkle over the top.

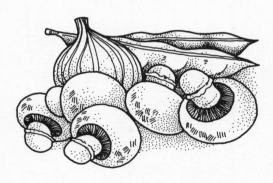

## LEEKS BAKED WITH TOMATOES

4-6 leeks
3 tablespoonsful nutter or margarine
4 large ripe tomatoes
Dash of basil
2 teaspoonsful cornflour
$\frac{1}{2}$ cupful thick cream
Salt and pepper

Wash and trim the leeks then cut into 1-inch lengths. Put the nutter in a shallow heat-proof dish and add the leeks. Bake at 375°F (190°C/Gas Mark 5) for 5 minutes. Skin the tomatoes and cut them in halves, crosswise. Sprinkle them with salt and pepper and arrange on top of the leeks. Sprinkle with a little basil. Bake for 5 minutes on one side, then turn over and cook until done. Blend the cornflour with the cream. Lift the tomatoes onto a hot dish and pour the cornflour and cream over the leeks. Season and cook until the sauce has thickened, then serve the leeks round the tomatoes.

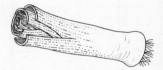

## LEEK AND POTATO PIE

2 large floury potatoes
1 small onion
3 tablespoonsful cream
Nutter or margarine or olive oil
Salt and pepper
Browned breadcrumbs
2 measuring cupsful minced leeks
$\frac{1}{2}$ pt. (275ml) sour cream
1 beaten egg

Peel the potatoes and onion and dice them. Put them into a thick pan and cover with $\frac{1}{4}$ cupful of water, salt and pepper. When soft, mash as they are and add the cream and some nutter or oil. Grease a sandwich tin and cover the sides and bottom with crumbs, then spread the potato on top as if it were a pastry lining. *Sauté* the leeks in nutter or oil for about 5 minutes or until just tender. Season with salt and pepper and spread on top of the potato. Season the sour cream and mix with the egg and spread on the leeks. Bake at 375°F (190°C/Gas Mark 5) until the cream is a pale primrose colour. Serve at once.

## STUFFED LETTUCE LEAVES

Large lettuce leaves
Boiling water
4 tablespoonful cream
1 cupful minced *sautéed* mushrooms
½ cupful breadcrumbs
1 cupful cooked brown rice
1 beaten egg
3 tablespoonful sherry
½ cupful minced parsley
3 tablespoonful finely-minced chives

Dip the lettuce leaves in boiling water for not more than 2 minutes or less. Drain them. Put a little nutter or oil on the bottom of a baking dish. Mix the mushrooms, breadcrumbs, rice, egg, sherry, parsley and chives. Put a little on each lettuce leaf and roll up into parcels with the ends tucked in and then fasten them with cocktail sticks or tie them with string so that they do not come undone. Put the rolls in the dish on the oil and see that they are close together. Bake for 25 minutes at 350°F (175°C/Gas Mark 4), then lift very carefully onto a hot dish and pour the liquid from the pan over them.

## MARTINIQUE YELLOW MARROW

1¾ lb (875g) yellow or golden fleshed marrow
1 medium-sized onion, minced
*Bouquet garni*: 1 bay leaf, 6 sprigs parsley
½ pt. (275ml) rich white sauce
2 beaten egg yolks
2 tablespoonful grated Swiss cheese
Salt and cayenne pepper
Buttered crumbs

Use any marrow with golden flesh, wipe it then cut into pieces. Put into a pan with just enough boiling water to prevent the marrow from sticking to the bottom of the pan. Add the chopped onion, the *bouquet garni*, tied with cotton, and cook for about 15 minutes. Drain and discard the seasonings. Make the white sauce and beat in the egg yolks, cheese and season highly with salt and cayenne pepper. Mix with the marrow and put into a baking dish. Cover with some more cheese mixed with an equal quantity of buttered crumbs. Bake at 300°F (145°C/Gas Mark 2) for about 35 minutes. Serve at once.

## MARROW CORN BREAD

¾ cupful cooked, mashed marrow, yellow for
   choice
1 level tablespoonful bicarbonate of soda
1 tablespoonful nutter
½ pt. (275ml) buttermilk
½ pt. (275ml) soured cream
2 tablespoonsful brown sugar
¾ lb (325g) cornmeal
1 teaspoonful salt
2 eggs, separated

Mix the soda with a tablespoonful of cold
water. Mix all the other ingredients
except the egg whites, then add the stiffly
beaten egg whites at the last. Bake in a
greased bread tin for half an hour at 350°F
(175°C/Gas Mark 4). Serve sliced and hot
with nutter or margarine.

## BAKED VEGETABLE
## MARROW WITH ORANGE

4 cupful peeled, cubed yellow marrow
1 tablespoonful grated orange rind
½ cupful orange juice
2 tablespoonsful cream
1½ tablespoonsful nutter
1 tablespoonful honey
Salt and pepper
Pinch ground ginger

Bake the marrow or steam it for 15
minutes. Mash the marrow. Mix all the
other ingredients together and bring to
just below boiling point, then mix in the
marrow. The mixture should be the
consistency of fluffy mashed potatoes. Eat
when hot or fry in small cakes when cold.

## FRIED VEGETABLE MARROW
## WITH CARAMEL SAUCE

2 Crookneck marrows
2 tablespoonsful light golden syrup
Salt and pepper
Cooking oil and nutter for frying
¼ cupful cream
Grated cheese for garnish

Do not peel the marrows unless the skin
seems coarse, just scrape and uncover the
pale green skin that is underneath. If
really young, do not peel or de-seed. Slice
the marrows ¾ inch thick. Mix the syrup
with oil and nutter in a pan and glaze the
marrow slices in it, almost burning them
(if you do not like the sweetness of golden
syrup, use corn syrup which is not sweet).
Pepper and salt the slices and cook
uncovered until just tender. This will take
only about 8 minutes.
   Empty the marrow into a serving dish.
Put the cream into the pan, let it come to
the boil, dissolve all the residue, and stir
often. The cream will turn a rich brown.
Then pour over the marrow and top with
cheese. The cheese may be omitted and
cornflake crumbs used instead. Serve at
once.

# VEGETABLE MARROW CASSEROLE

2½ lb (1¼kg) any kind of marrow
3 tablespoonsful nutter or margarine
¾ cupful minced onion
2 teaspoonsful cornflour
Salt and pepper
1 level teaspoonful curry powder
1 tablespoonful brown sugar
1 tablespoonful lemon juice
½ pt. (275ml) thin cream
Grated cheese for garnish

Grease a baking dish generously with oil, nutter or margarine. Do not peel the marrow unless the skin seems tough; cut it into ½-inch slices and put alternate layers of marrow and onion in the dish and dot with fat. Cover and bake until tender at 350°F (175°C/Gas Mark 4).

Mix the curry powder, sugar and lemon juice with the cornflour and cream. Cook over low heat to thicken and then pour over the marrow and put back into the oven. When baked, season with salt and pepper. Do not add the salt until after it is baked because if you do it will draw out too much water. Sprinkle with cheese and serve.

# VEGETABLE MARROW WITH DILL SAUCE

2 lb (about 1kg) yellow vegetable marrow
2 tablespoonsful chopped onion tops
4 tablespoonsful chopped green pepper
Pinch nutmeg
¼ pt. (150ml) thin cream
2 teaspoonsful cornflour
Olive oil or nutter
Seat salt and pepper

**Dill Sauce**
1 handful fresh dill or chervil, stems chopped finely
¼ cupful thin cream
2 teaspoonsful cornflour
Salt and pepper

Prepare the marrow with the skin on, unless it is an old one, in which case slice into ½-inch slices. *Sauté* the onion tops and green pepper in oil or nutter, or both mixed. When nearly tender, add the marrow and seasonings and cook until tender. This will take from 10-15 minutes for a young marrow. Make the chosen sauce in the usual way.

# MARROW AND PINEAPPLE

Small marrows or courgettes
Fresh pineapple, sliced thinly
Salt and pepper
Spring onions, chopped
Olive oil

**Dressing**
¼ cupful cream mixed with ½ cupful grated cheese or cottage cheese

Boil the marrows whole for about 10 minutes. Then cut in halves lengthwise and scoop out the seeds. Fill the cavities with pineapple and sprinkle with salt and spring onions. Put the marrows in a tin with a little oil and cook for about 20 minutes at 325°F (160°C/Gas Mark 3). Make the sauce hot and pour over the cooked marrows. The quantities of sauce given will do for four marrows.

## ZUCCHINI PROVENÇALE

2 lb (about 1kg) zucchini
1 medium onion, sliced
4 tablespoonsful vegetable oil
4 large tomatoes, peeled and de-seeded
1 green pepper, finely chopped
1 clove garlic
Salt and pepper
Mixed chopped parsley and Parmesan cheese
　garnish

Wash the zucchini, peel it and cut into cubes. *Sauté* the onion in the oil, add the tomatoes cut in quarters and the green pepper, crush the garlic slightly and add it. Season with salt and pepper and cook for 15 minutes over low heat. Lift out the garlic and add the zucchini, cover and cook until the zucchini is tender. Put on to a hot serving dish and garnish.

## MUSHROOMS WITH ARTICHOKE BOTTOMS

8 large artichoke bottoms (tinned)
8 large mushrooms
¾ cupful fine dry breadcrumbs
1 clove garlic, chopped
4 tablespoonsful chopped parsley
½ cupful olive oil
Salt and cayenne pepper

Do not peel the mushrooms unless they are dirty and black, just wash them quickly and cut the stalks level with the caps.

*Sauté* the caps and the artichoke bottoms in half the oil. Cover the pan and do not break the vegetables. Then lift out of the pan very carefully and put a little oil on each artichoke bottom. *Sauté* the breadcrumbs in another pan, with the chopped mushroom stalks, garlic and parsley using the rest of the oil. Arrange the artichoke bottoms on the dish and cover each one with a mushroom cap, gills up and fill the mushrooms with the breadcrumb mixture. Sprinkle with salt and pepper. Heat for 10 minutes at 325°F (160°C/Gas Mark 3).

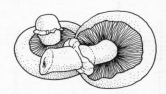

## MUSHROOMS WITH MADEIRA

12 oz. (350g) mushrooms
¼ pt. (150ml) Madeira
1 pt. (550ml) milk
1 dessertspoonful 81 per cent flour
1 dessertspoonful olive oil or cooking fat
3 bay leaves
Cayenne pepper and salt

Do not peel the mushrooms unless they look dirty. Cut off the stalks near the caps. Chop the stalks and add them to the milk and bay leaves and season with salt and pepper. Boil until the milk is grey, then add half the Madeira and remove from the heat. Make a *roux* from the fat and flour and when it bubbles, strain the milk onto it, stir and cook until it thickens. If the mushrooms are button ones, add them whole. Heat the sauce, add the mushrooms, cook gently then taste for seasonings and add any needed (some cooks like to add a little mace or nutmeg at this point). Add the rest of the Madeira and cook until the sauce is thick. Pour into individual dishes and serve with thin brown toast.

## STUFFED MUSHROOMS

8 very large mushrooms
1 lb (450g) mixed size mushrooms
6 oz. (175g) breadcrumbs (brown bread)
2 shallots
2 tablespoonsful chopped parsley or chervil
1 egg
4 oz. (100g) margarine
Juice of 1 small lemon
Cayenne pepper and sea salt

Peel the large mushrooms and cut off the stalks. Put the other mushrooms and the stalks through the mincer. Soak the breadcrumbs in enough water just to moisten them. Soften the shallots (chopped) in fat or oil. Put 2 oz. (50g) of margarine in a pan and melt it, add the minced mushrooms, breadcrumbs, parsley or chervil, shallots, pepper and salt. Cook over low heat for 8-10 minutes until the mixture looks drier. Take off the heat and beat in the egg and lemon juice.

Arrange the mushrooms on a greased baking dish, pile the stuffing on them, sprinkle a few crumbs on top and dot with margarine. Bake at 350°F (170°C/Gas Mark 4) and watch carefully. Take out of the oven as soon as they look done, the time depending on the size of the mushrooms.

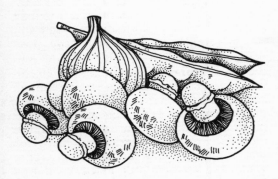

## SPRING ONIONS AND BROWN RICE

1½ cupful brown rice
1 pt. (550ml) vegetable stock
3 tablespoonsful sultanas
1 teaspoonful turmeric
4 tablespoonsful sherry
2 tablespoonsful pine nuts (pignolias)
½ cupful minced spring onions
1 tablespoonful preserved ginger, minced

Put the rice in a pan with the stock and turmeric, cover and cook over low heat for 45 minutes. Turn off the heat and leave to stand covered for 10 minutes more. Steep the sultanas in the sherry while the rice is cooking. Add the sultanas and the rest of the ingredients. This dish may be served with scrambled eggs or on its own.

## ONIONS MADÈRE

1½ lb (675g) small onions, not pickling ones
Brown sugar or honey
Pinch of mace
Nutter or margarine
2 tablespoonsful currants
⅓ cupful Madeira
Salt and pepper
4 tablespoonsful seeded raisins

Put the honey in a frying pan and heat it. Peel the onions and glaze them in the pan, then put them in a shallow ovenware dish and sprinkle with mace, a dash of salt and pepper, the Madeira, raisins and currants. Cover tightly and bake for about 40 minutes at 350°F (175°C/Gas Mark 4). Look at the dish after 20 minutes and if a lot of juice has run out of the ingredients, leave off the cover.

## ONION PIE

**Pastry**
2 oz. (50g) 81 per cent flour
2 oz. (50g) wholemeal flour
3 oz. (75g) margarine (or Trex)
Water

Make the pastry in the usual way, adding a little sea salt.

**Filling**
2½ cupful thinly sliced onions
1 cupful soured cream
2 tablespoonsful nutter
Salt and cayenne pepper
Dash of powdered cloves (optional)
2 large fresh eggs
1 dessertspoonful 81 per cent flour

Cook the onions in the nutter, salt, pepper and cloves in a thick frying pan for about 20 minutes, until they are just tender. Roll out the pastry to fit an 8- or 9-inch pie plate and spread the onions, etc., evenly on it as it lines the plate. Beat the eggs and flour together, add salt and then mix in the sour cream and pour on top of the onions. Do not stir it in. Trim the pastry edges and put into the oven at 375°F (190°C/Gas Mark 5) and cook for 15 minutes, then turn the heat down to 325°F (160°C/Gas Mark 3) for 8 minutes until the pastry is golden and the filling set. Serve hot.

## ONION SOUFFLÉ

1½ lb (675g) small onions
Pinch of cloves (optional)
Salt and cayenne pepper
1½ tablespoonsful nutter or margarine
4 tablespoonsful 81 per cent flour
¼ pt. (150ml) cream
5 egg yolks
3 egg whites
Cheese or tomato sauce

Peel the onions, slice them very thinly and cook them in ⅓ cupful water with the salt, pepper and cloves. When tender, put through the blender. You should have 2 cupsful of onion *purée*. Make a sauce from the nutter, flour and cream; when thick, remove from the heat and add the beaten egg yolks. Beat well and then add the onion *purée*. Whip the egg whites until very stiff and fold into the mixture. Put in a well-greased *soufflé* dish or casserole and bake at 350°F (175°C/Gas Mark 4) for 25-30 minutes. A tomato sauce may be made from a tin of tomato sauce or *puréed* tomatoes mixed with an equal amount of soured cream. Heat the tomato and add the cream, but do not try to heat the sour cream or it will curdle.

## ONION AND APPLE BAKE

3 large Spanish onions
5 large cooking apples
Nutter, salt and pepper
Brown sugar
Pinch of cinnamon
⅓ cupful onion water

Peel the onions and cut them up small. Cook in as little water as possible with the nutter, salt and pepper until just not quite tender. Do not let them get mushy. Peel and core the apples and slice them thinly. Grease a fireproof dish and put alternate layers of onion and apple in it and sprinkle each layer with a little sugar and cinnamon mixed and add pepper and salt. Tiny flakes of margarine or nutter may be added if liked. Add the water in which the onions were cooked, cover tightly and bake for an hour at 350°F (170°C/Gas Mark 4) for half the time and at 325°F (160°C/Gas Mark 3) for the last half hour. If there seems to be a lot of liquid in the dish, leave off the cover for the last 15 minutes.

# ONIONS, BAKED AND CREAMED

4 large Spanish onions
Sea salt and pepper
Pinch of cloves or mace
Some light brown sugar

**Sauce**
½ cupful onion water
3 tablespoonful brown or 81 per cent flour
¼ pt. (150ml) cream or undiluted tinned milk
1½ tablespoonful nutter
Salt and pepper

Peel the onions and if they are very large cut them in halves. Cook in boiling salted water until they are half done and still very firm. Put in a large greased baking dish, cut sides up, if sliced in halves, sprinkle them with mixed salt, pepper, spice and sugar. Make a sauce from the flour, spice nutter and onion water, then add the cream. When thickened, spoon it over the onions and bake at 325°F (160°C/Gas Mark 3) for about 35 minutes or until the onions are tender. Grated cheese or parsley may be sprinkled over the top.

# ONION AND BROAD BEAN BAKE

18 small white skinned onions
3 tablespoonful nutter
1 dessertspoonful 81 per cent flour
½ pt. (275ml) water
*Bouquet garni* of 2 pieces green celery leaves,
    1 sprig thyme, 4 sprigs parsley and 1 bay leaf
    tied together
1 pt. (550ml) measure of broad beans
Salt and pepper

Wash and peel the onions. Melt the nutter in a casserole, add the onions and *sauté* them until they are golden. Sprinkle with flour. Add the water and *bouquet garni*, season with salt and pepper and simmer gently in a covered casserole for 15 minutes. Then add the beans and simmer until tender. Shake the casserole often so that the contents do not burn. Serve in the casserole.

# SOUR CREAM AND ONION PIE

3 tablespoonful nutter
2½ lb (1¼kg) sliced Spanish onions
½ pt. (275ml) sour cream
4 tablespoonful sherry
3 beaten eggs
Salt and cayenne pepper
Dash of thyme and mace
½ lb (225g) flaky pastry

Melt the nutter in a thick saucepan and stir in the thinly-sliced onions and cook over low heat until they are transparent. Remove from the heat and leave until quite cold. Mix the sour cream and the sherry with the well-beaten eggs and stir into the cold onions, season with salt, pepper, thyme and mace. Line a plate or tin with flaky pastry and fill with the onion mixture. Make a lattice of pastry trimmings and put over the top. Trim neatly and bake at 350°F (175°C/Gas Mark 4) until the filling is firm and the pastry delicate golden. Serve as hot as possible.

## CURRIED FRENCH ONION DUMPLINGS

2 measuring cupsful of sifted 81 per cent flour
1½ teaspoonsful baking powder
½ teaspoonful salt
1 level teaspoonful curry powder
Pinch each of mace, thyme and cloves
4-5 oz. (100-150g) nutter or margarine
½ cupful rich milk

**Filling**
6 large onions, baked in their skins at 375°F
    (190°C/Gas Mark 5)
Nutter
Hot tomato sauce

To make the pastry, sift the flour, salt and baking powder three times then rub in the fat until like fine crumbs; add the herbs and curry powder and mix well. Then add the milk to make a soft dough. Turn out and knead for about 6 turns. Roll out ⅛ inch thick and cut out six rounds large enough to cover the onions. Take the skins off the baked onions (it takes about an hour to cook them), rub them with nutter or margarine and sprinkle with a little salt. Dampen the edges of the pastry circles and put an onion on each one; wrap the dough round the onion and seal carefully. Grease a baking dish and put the dumplings in it close together with the sealed edges underneath. Brush them with fat and bake for 20-25 minutes at 450°F (230°C/Gas Mark 8). Serve very hot with tomato sauce.

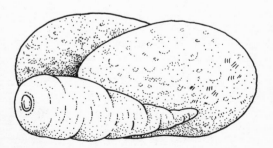

## SMOTHERED ONIONS WITH ALMONDS

36 small onions
4 tablespoonsful nutter or best margarine
6 oz. (175g) whole blanched almonds
1 tablespoonful dark brown sugar
1 level teaspoonful salt
Pinch of cayenne pepper and nutmeg

Wash and peel the onions. Melt the butter in an ovenware dish with a lid, put the almonds in it, season with sugar, salt, pepper and spices, blend carefully and then add the onions and stir until covered with the mixture. Cover the dish and bake at 350°F (175°C/Gas Mark 4) for about one hour. Shake the dish frequently. The onions should be very tender and the almonds golden brown.

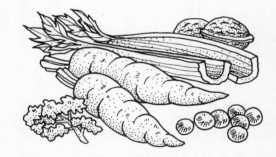

## POTATO PANCAKES (1)

1 lb (450g) potatoes, grated raw
2 tablespoonsful of left-over mashed potatoes
2 tablespoonsful milk
2 eggs
1 teaspoonful grated onion
Salt and cayenne pepper

Mix all the ingredients together and fry in cooking fat or oil half an inch deep. Turn once and drain on soft paper. Now comes the surprise: put the pancakes on a hot dish and sprinkle with a little sugar, then *flambé* with schnapps or kirsh: be generous with the spirit. Do not forget to heat it.

## POTATO PANCAKES (2)

5-6 floury potatoes to make 2 cupsful
   riced potatoes
2 tablespoonsful chopped parsley
1 cupful soft breadcrumbs
1 small onion, grated
2 beaten eggs
2 dessertspoonsful milk
¼ pt. (150ml) cream

Mix all the ingredients together in the order given. Make into small flat cakes and roll in crumbs. Brown on both sides in hot fat or oil. Serve with one of the ready-made nut rissoles or loaves.

    Whenever it is possible, potatoes should be cooked in their skins. A medium-sized potato has the same number of calories as an orange and is a valuable part of our diet.

    Baked potatoes are always popular and even little new ones may be cooked this way. The best way to cook them is to boil them (after scrubbing) only just enough to heat them through; then drain and bake in a hot oven. Old potatoes take from 40-60 minutes started at 375°F (190°C/Gas Mark 5) with the heat lowered after 20 minutes. Small new potatoes should take about half as long. Baked potatoes lend themselves to being stuffed. After they have been baked, split the skins along one side and scoup out most of the pulp, mix with the chosen ingredients, refill the skins and put them back in the oven to heat. Here are a few ideas for stuffing.

## LEEK STUFFING

Mince some leeks and *sauté* them in nutter, season with salt and pepper and mix in some cream, then blend with the potato pulp.

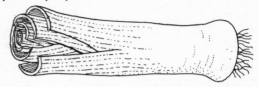

## NUT STUFFING

Mix some peanut butter or ground almonds with salt and pepper, add some hot cream, a little margarine or nutter and if liked, a beaten egg.

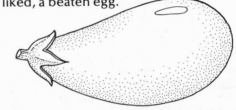

## HERB STUFFING

Mince some fresh parsley, basil, tarragon, chervil and chives and blend with margarine, hot cream, salt and pepper.

## CHEESE STUFFING

To 1 cupful of grated Cheddar cheese, add 1 teaspoonful thyme, hot cream to blend, salt and pepper, melted nutter and then sprinkle the tops with chopped parsley.

## MUSHROOM STUFFING

Mix chopped *sautéed* mushrooms with chives, hot cream, tarragon and margarine.

I hope this gives you some ideas but they by no means exhaust the materials.

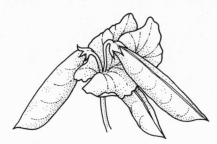

## POTATO PIE

8 oz. (225g) 81 per cent flour
½ teaspoonful salt
1 heaped teaspoonful baking powder
5 oz. (150g) nutter and cooking fat mixed
2 tablespoonsful soft margarine
Milk to mix

**Filling**
4-5 potatoes (2¼ cupsful, mashed)
Salt and pepper
8 oz. (225g) creamed cottage cheese
¼ cupful sour cream
1 small onion, grated
1 beaten egg

Make the pastry first by sifting the dry ingredients. Cut in the mixed fats, add salt and enough milk to make a soft but not sticky dough (like a scone dough). Roll it out and dot with the 2 tablespoonsful of soft margarine, fold over, roll out again and line an 8-inch plate with it. To prepare the filling, boil the potatoes in their jackets, skin and mash them and blend all the ingredients together. Fill the pastry with this and bake for 10 minutes at 400°F (200°C/Gas Mark 6) then turn the heat to 325°F (160°C/Gas Mark 3) and bake for another 20 minutes. Serve poached eggs and tomato sauce with this.

## POTATO AND ALMOND SOUFFLÉ

2½ cupsful mashed potatoes, cooked as above
Dash of mace
Salt and pepper
½ cupful ground almonds
½ cupful thin cream
4 eggs, separated

Mix all the ingredients except the egg whites. Beat the egg white to the stiff peak stage, then fold into the first mixture. Bake in a greased *soufflé* dish with the ground almonds sprinkled on top for 20 minutes at 375°F (190°C/Gas Mark 5). Other ingredients may be added if liked, such as mashed turnip, swede or carrot instead of the same amount of potato. A few peas add colour.

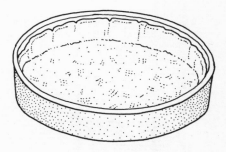

## POTATOES CHANTILLY

4 large floury potatoes
1 cupful whipped cream
Pinch of nutmeg
Salt and cayenne pepper
½ cupful Parmesan cheese (grated)

Boil, skin and rice the potatoes in a greased ovenware dish. Whip the cream and season it; spread the cream on top of the potatoes, sprinkle the cheese on top and bake at 375°F (190°C/Gas Mark 5) for 7-8 minutes.

## PASTA AL PESTO

1 clove of garlic
1 cupful of basil
1 tablespoonful pine nuts (pignolias)
6 sprigs of oregano
¼ cupful pecorino cheese, grated
Good pinch of cayenne pepper
½ cupful olive oil
Spaghetti or any other pasta, cooked

Grind the herbs in a pestle or put them in the blender. Then add the oil slowly until you have a sauce that will pour easily. It should be a lovely green colour. Add salt and cayenne pepper to taste, pour over the hot pasta and mix well lifting it with care. Hand the cheese separately.

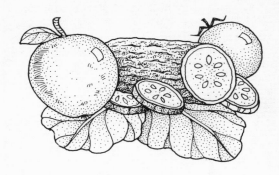

## PASTA AND PEAS WITH SAUCE

3 tablespoonsful minced raw onion
3 tablespoonsful olive oil
1 teaspoonful dried thyme
1 teaspoonful basil
Salt and pepper
2 lb (about 1kg) green peas
10-12 oz. (275-350g) spaghetti or macaroni
3 tablespoonsful nutter
Salt and pepper
Grated cheese for the top

**Sauce**
3 cloves of garlic
2 tablespoonsful pignolas
¼ cupful Parmesan cheese or Romano cheese
Olive oil
Salt and pepper

*Sauté* the onion in the oil, add the herbs and seasonings, then the peas and simmer until tender, with about 2 tablespoonsful hot water. To make the sauce: crush the garlic and mix with the nuts and cheese, then put through the blender with the oil, salt and pepper. Boil the chosen pasta for 10-12 minutes in salted water, then drain it and mix in the nutter. Mix the peas and pasta and then stir in the sauce. Serve at once with a bowl of grated cheese.

## BAKED LASAGNE

First boil the strips or sheets of lasagne in plenty of salted boiling water until tender. Arrange in a dish with thin layers of filling between. Pour a sauce over the top and bake until hot at about 350°F (175°C/Gas Mark 4). Cheese and spinach are favourite fillings; tomato sauce is also good.

## STUFFED CRÊPES

The great objection to making pancakes is that they leave such a strong smell of hot fat or oil behind them that can even permeate the whole house. The remedy is simple: just add a little oil to the pancake batter. After doing this you need grease the frying pan once only, for the first pancake, and no more.

6 oz. (175g) 81 per cent flour
½ pt. (275ml) milk
½ teaspoonful salt
2 eggs
1 tablespoonful cooking fat or oil

Cook the pancakes in a pan not more than 6 inches in diameter. Sift the flour and salt, drop in the eggs and mix a little, then add the milk and oil and mix just to blend. To beat a batter is to make tough pancakes or Yorkshire pudding; any little lumps will disappear in the cooking. Leave the batter to stand for half an hour or longer. Then grease the bottom of the frying pan and pour in enough batter (about 1 tablespoonful) to make a thin cake and turn once only. Keep hot on a tea towel or between pieces of soft paper. When all the pancakes are cooked (you will have about 14) fill each one with the chosen filling, roll up and put close together in a fireproof dish, cover with either sauce or grated cheese and brown lightly under the grill. Any stuffing is good; sweet stuffings make a first class pudding. For a savoury filling try spinach and egg cooked together; *sautéed* mushrooms; soft cheese; tomatoes; cream cheese; boiled chopped onions or fried ones; leeks and so on. Let your imagination run free.

## GNOCCHI DI SEMOLINA

1 pt. (550ml) milk
4 oz. (100g) semolina
⅛ teaspoonful salt
3 oz. (75g) grated Parmesan cheese
1 beaten egg yolk
3 tablespoonsful nutter or best margarine

Bring the milk to the boil using a wooden spoon and a thick saucepan and sprinkle in the semolina a little at a time, stirring constantly. Lower the heat when it begins to thicken, stir all the time and cook for 10 minutes at least. Take off the heat and add 1 tablespoonful of the fat, the egg and salt, beat and stir vigorously, then pour onto a marble slab or kitchen table top. It is best to dampen the surface slightly first. Smooth out the mixture to about ¾-inch thickness and leave to cool for not less than one hour. Then cut with a sharp knife into little squares or lozenges: to cut into rounds is very wasteful. Take a large shallow ovenware dish and oil it well. Cover with a layer of gnocchi putting the pieces at least ¼ inch apart. Sprinkle with the Parmesan cheese, dot with fat and repeat the layers. Put in the oven at 350°F (175°C/Gas Mark 4) and cook until pale brown on top. Serve with a favourite sauce.

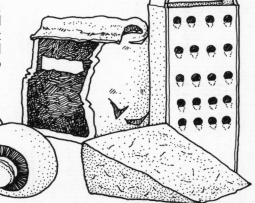

# NOODLES

¼ lb (100g) flour
1 egg yolk
Pinch of salt
A little milk or water

Mix the flour and salt. Beat the egg yolk just to blend it and then mix with the flour. Mix well and add a little milk or water if the paste is too stiff and will not bind. It will be a little sticky so knead it until it is smooth then leave it in a cool place for about half an hour. Roll it out very thinly, as thinly as possible, and then make it into a roll and cut into narrow ribbons with a very sharp knife. Let the noodles dry and then store them in an airtight tin until needed. Cook them in boiling salted water until they are tender: these home-made ones will take only a few minutes to cook. Then use with sauces or just grated cheese.

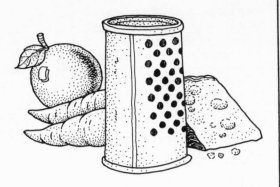

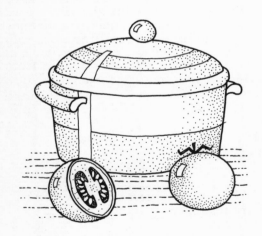

## FRIED CRISPY NOODLES

These morsels are so good as a garnish with almost any savoury dish.

Boil the noodles; do not let them get mushy. Have some hot fat ready, three quarters of an inch of fat or oil is enough, drop the noodles into it and fry until crisp.

## TUSCAN RICE

1½ cupsful raw rice (3 cupsful when cooked)
3 tablespoonsful margarine
3 egg yolks, beaten
⅔ cupful Parmesan cheese, grated
Pinch of cayenne pepper
1 tablespoonful lemon juice

Boil the rice in a large pan of salted water. When the rice is tender, but not mushy, drain it and keep ½ cupful of the water. Wash the rice well under running water. Add the egg yolks to the ½ cupful of rice water, then beat in the lemon juice and pepper and pour over the rice, mix in half the cheese and all the margarine. Mix well and serve in a large dish; the rest of the cheese and small pieces of lemon may be served in a separate dish. Rice done this way makes a good foundation for creamed eggs or root vegetables.

Pilafs are made a little differently. Firstly, the rice is fried in hot oil; liquid is then added and the rice finishes cooking in the oven. It is important to use the right type of rice. Some rice will absorb a cupful of liquid to a cupful of rice while others will take 2 cupsful of liquid to 1 of rice. Use stock as the liquid, not water. One cupful of raw rice will on average make 3 or 4 cupsful cooked.

## EASTERN RICE

3 cupsful raw long grain rice
4½ cupsful vegetable stock
1 onion, minced
1 onion, ringed
1 clove garlic, minced
20-30 blanched almonds
2 hard-boiled eggs
2 bay leaves
3 tablespoonsful margarine or olive oil
10 whole peppercorns
¼ teaspoonful saffron
Salt

Melt the fat or heat the oil in a large strong frying pan and then put in the almonds and cook until they begin to brown. Add the minced garlic and onion. When the onion is transparent, add the rice and go on cooking until the rice is brown. Turn into a large casserole, add the stock, peppercorns and bay leaves and mix in the saffron. *Do not stir.* When the mixture starts to boil, cover and transfer to the oven and bake for 20 minutes at 350°F (175°C/Gas Mark 4). Dip the onion rings in flour and fry in hot oil until brown and crisp. Pile the rice high on a hot dish and garnish with hard-boiled eggs and onion rings. A curry sauce may be served separately but there is no need for it: the dish is excellent as it is.

## JAMAICA RICE AND BEANS

1¼ cupsful dried beans of choice
⅔ cupful desiccated coconut
1 large onion, diced
2 cloves of crushed garlic
1 teaspoonful of Worcester sauce
1 tablespoonful dried mixed herbs
1½ tablespoonsful dark brown sugar
2 cupsfuls washed brown rice
Salt and black pepper

Wash the beans and soak them in 1 qt. (1¼l) of cold water for not less than 12 hours, more if possible. Then simmer them in the same water for about 2 hours or until they are tender, strain off the water and pour it on to the coconut. Leave to stand for 5 minutes, to infuse, then strain and squeeze out all the liquid and discard the coconut. There should be 2½ cupsful of liquid; if less, add water.

Fry the onion in a little hot oil until slightly coloured then add all the other ingredients including the rice and beans. Pour the coconut water over all, cover tightly and cook over very low heat for 45 minutes. It should be a little damper than rice cooked for curry. These amounts will serve a lot of people but it is just as good when warmed up.

## CALIFORNIAN RICE AND OLIVES

1¼ cupsful raw rice
2 cloves of garlic
2 tablespoonsful each of olive oil and nutter
4½ cupsful tomato juice
¾ cupful sliced black olives
2 teaspoonsful each of chili powder and salt
1 teaspoonful dried dill

Mix the oil and nutter and brown the rice and garlic in it. Lift out the garlic and add the tomato juice, olives, chili powder, salt and herb. Pour into a greased baking dish and bake covered for one hour, or until the rice is tender, at 350°F (175°C/Gas Mark 4), by which time all moisture should have been absorbed.

# ORANGE AND THYME RICE

2 small chopped onions
2 tablespoonful nutter
1 cupful orange juice
1 cupful water
1 tablespoonful grated orange rind
½ teaspoonful salt
½ teaspoonful dried thyme
1 cupful raw brown rice

Melt the fat in a frying pan and *sauté* the onion in it, when it is soft, add the orange juice and water, the orange rind, salt and thyme. Bring to the boil and add the rice slowly; stir for a second or two, cover the pan and simmer for 25-30 minutes until the rice is tender but firm.

# CURRIED RICE SOUFFLÉ

1 cupful dry white wine
1 cupful grated Swiss cheese
1 teaspoonful made mustard
Pinch of cayenne pepper
½ teaspoonful salt
2 teaspoonsful nutter
1 teaspoonful grated onion
3 eggs, separated
½ cupful boiled rice
1½ teaspoonsful curry powder (more if preferred)
6 large individual *soufflé* dishes

Heat the wine but do not boil it. Lift the pan from the heat and add the cheese, mustard, pepper, salt and the nutter kneaded with the onion. Partially melt the cheese then pour the mixture over the lightly-beaten egg yolks. Mix the rice and curry powder and stir into the first mixture. Taste for seasonings then fold in the stiffly beaten egg whites. Fill *soufflé* dishes only three quarters full. Bake at 400°F (200°C/Gas Mark 6) for 20 minutes or until the *soufflés* are puffed and golden brown. Serve without delay.

# GLAZED PARSNIPS

6 large parsnips
2 tablespoonsful butter or vegetable oil
2 tablespoonsful orange juice
3 tablespoonsful brown sugar or clear honey
Salt and pepper

Steam or boil the parsnips in a little salted water, use the smallest amount possible. Do not peel them first, just wash them. When they are tender, skin them and cut in halves lengthwise; if very long, cut across as well. Put the fat or oil, the orange juice, sugar or honey in a thick frying pan and, when melted and mixed, add the parsnips, then turn them often and cook until glazed. Add more fat and sugar if needed.

# PARSNIP PIE

1 lb (450g) parsnips
1 lb (450g) shelled green peas
1 cupful cubed cooked potatoes
2 dessertspoonsful cornflour
$\frac{1}{2}$ pt. (275ml) thick cream
2 tablespoonsful grated onion
Dash of mace
$\frac{1}{2}$ cupful vegetable water
Grated cheese for the top, if liked

Cook all the vegetables separately in as little salted water as possible. Reserve the parsnip and pea water for the sauce, but do not use the potato water. Skin the parsnips. Mix the cream and cornflour and cook to thicken it; then add the onion, mace, vegetable water, salt and pepper. Make pastry from any of the pastry recipes and line a 9-inch pie plate with part of it. Prick all over and line the pastry with paper weighed down with cooking beans, bake for 15 minutes at 400°F (200°C/Gas Mark 6).

Remove beans and paper and arrange the vegetables on the pastry and pour the sauce on top. Make a lattice of pastry strips, put them over the top of the filling and put back in the oven just to brown it. Grate the cheese on top if used. Serve hot.

# GREEN PEAS AND CHEESE

$\frac{1}{4}$ cupful olive oil
4 spring onions, minced
1 clove of crushed garlic
2 lb (about 1kg) green peas
1 teaspoonful honey
1 teaspoonful chervil, chopped stalks, whole leaves
$\frac{1}{3}$ cupful grated Parmesan cheese
Salt and pepper

Put the olive oil in a thick saucepan and *sauté* the garlic and minced onion in it, then add the peas, honey, seasonings and 3 tablespoonsful of water. Cover and cook gently until just tender, then add the crushed chervil stalks. Serve when ready sprinkled with cheese and chervil leaves.

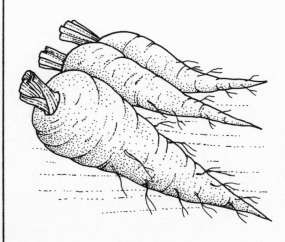

# PEA SOUFFLÉ WITH ALMONDS

2 lb (about 1kg) green peas cooked in nutter
    and a spot of water
3 tablespoonsful milk
2 tablespoonsful 81 per cent flour
¼ cupful toasted almonds, minced
¼ pt. (150ml) cream
2 drops of almond or ratafia essence
3 eggs, separated
Salt and pepper

Cook the peas as above and then mash
them or process in a blender. Add the
flour. There should be 2 cupsful of *purée*.
Mix the almonds and cream and bring just
to boiling point. Add the pea *pureé* and
essence and beat in the egg yolks. Beat
the egg whites to a stiff peak and fold into
the first mixture adding salt and pepper to
taste. Turn into a greased *soufflé* dish and
bake at 350°F (175°C/Gas Mark 4) for 30
minutes. Serve at once.

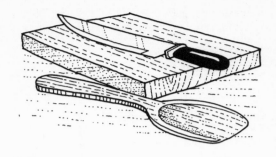

# BAKED PUMPKIN

2 lb (about 1kg) pumpkin
4 oz. (100g) nutter or margarine
3 oz. (75g) brown sugar
3 oz. (75g) chopped preserved ginger
Salt

Cut the pumpkin into serving pieces, peel
the wedges and discard the peel and
seeds. Melt the fat in a small pan; add the
sugar and ginger and melt together. Score
the pumpkin wedges with a knife and
spread the sugar, fat and ginger on it.
Sprinkle lightly with salt. Put the wedges
in a tin with ¼ inch of water in it and bake
at 350°F (175°C/Gas Mark 4) for 1½-2
hours, basting often.

# PEPPERS

Peppers, like tomatoes, came here from
America. The peppers given in the
following recipes are the sweet green, red
or yellow peppers, not the hot little
chillies. Some dishes call for skinned
peppers and this is the best way to
prepare them. Roast them in a hot oven
until the skins blister, or even blacken a
little, and then, while they are still hot, put
them into a paper bag or a steamer over
hot water. Cover tightly and steam for a
few minutes and then the skins will come
off quite easily. If peppers are wanted for
stuffing, boil them for 2-3 minutes, and
then drain them. Always remove seeds
and fibre.

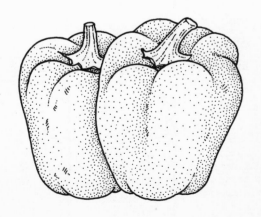

## TO STUFF RED, GREEN OR YELLOW PEPPERS

Select good-sized peppers. They may be stuffed whole but it is easier to cut them in halves to make cups or lengthwise to make boats. After the seeds and fibre have been removed, boil them for 3-4 minutes. Drain upside down and fill while still warm if they are to be baked, but if they are to be served cold, fill them when cold. If pre-cooked stuffing is used, there will be no need to cook the peppers more than 15-18 minutes. There are many suitable stuffings and left-over food is good served this way. Macaroni cheese makes a good stuffing; mixed sweet corn and onions make a colourful stuffing. Here are some more ideas.

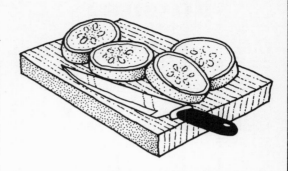

## BROAD BEAN AND MUSHROOM STUFFING

Mix equal quantities of broad beans, *sautéed* onion tops and chopped mushrooms. Cook for 15 minutes at 350°F (175°C/Gas Mark 4).

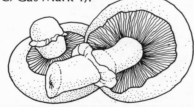

## ITALIAN STUFFING

*Sauté* some tiny bread cubes in olive oil with crushed garlic in it; add a few sliced black olives; bake for 30 minutes at 350°F (175°C/Gas Mark 4).

## PEPPERS, TOMATOES AND EGGS

4 large peppers, diced finely
2 cupsful finely diced onions
½ cupful olive oil
Salt and pepper
1½ teaspoonsful origano
Pinch of cumin
3 large ripe tomatoes, skinned and chopped
1 dessertspoonful brown sugar
5 eggs, beaten

Cook the onions in the olive oil, add the green peppers and cook until just tender. Add the salt, pepper, origano, cumin, tomatoes and brown sugar. Cover and cook until very soft for about half an hour at 350°F (175°C/Gas Mark 4). Then, if the sauce seems thin, uncover the dish or pan for the last 20 minutes to reduce the liquid. When quite soft add the beaten eggs and cook and stir on top of the cooker until they are set. Serve without delay.

## RATATOUILLE

1 small vegetable marrow, or courgette, sliced thickly, unpeeled
1 peeled cucumber, 4 inches long, sliced thinly
2 medium-sized tomatoes, cubed
2 onions, sliced from the top down, not ringed
3 sweet red peppers, seeded and cut in strips
1 small aubergine, peeled and chopped
4 oz. (100g) French beans
1 clove of garlic, chopped
1½ cupful olive oil
⅛ cupful chopped parsley
Good pinch each of dried basil and thyme
1 bay leaf
8 peppercorns

*Sauté* the onions and aubergine in half of the oil. When soft put them into a casserole with a tight lid, add the rest of the ingredients and bake at 350°F (175°C/Gas Mark 4) until the vegetables are tender (about half an hour). If the mixture looks sloppy remove the lid for the last 10 minutes of cooking time. Serve as a separate course with Parmesan cheese and toast spread with garlic butter.

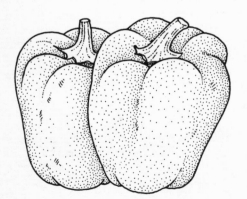

## BLACK RADISHES IN SAUCE

4 black radishes
4 tablespoonful minced onion
2 tablespoonful nutter or margarine
4 tablespoonful cold water
2 teaspoonful cornflour
¼ pt. (150ml) thin cream
½ teaspoonful turmeric
Salt and pepper

Scrape or peel the radishes and cut them in eighths lengthwise (cut them across if they are very long). *Sauté* the onions in the fat to soften them, then add the radishes, salt, pepper and water. Cover and steam until tender. In a pressure cooker it takes about 2½ minutes. Mix the cornflour with the turmeric and slake it with a little water. When the radishes are tender, add the cream and heat until it thickens.

## CHINESE RADISH CAKES

2 cupful shredded peeled black radishes
2 tablespoonful minced onion
1 beaten egg
¼ cupful ground rice
Salt and pepper
Oil for frying

The radishes should be about 8-inches long and 2-inches thick. Mix the first five ingredients and fry until brown in hot fat, then put them in the oven to cook for 15 minutes at 350°F (170°C/Gas Mark 4). Makes 6 cakes.

## SPINACH ROULADE

1 measuring cupful raw minced spinach

**Sauce**
1 tablespoonful 81 per cent flour
3 tablespoonsful nutter or margarine
½ pt. (275ml) milk
3 eggs, separated
Breadcrumbs
Salt and pepper

**Filling**
½ pt. (275ml) soured cream
1 cupful *sautéed* mushrooms

**Top**
3 tablespoonsful melted margarine and
 Parmesan cheese

Pack the spinach in the cup as firmly as
possible and squeeze out the juice. Melt
the fat, stir in the flour and add the milk
over low heat. Cook until it thickens and
then for 3 minutes longer. Add the salt
and pepper and beaten egg yolks. A little
herb such as basil may be added if liked.
Now mix in the spinach and fold in the
stiffly beaten egg whites. Put a piece of
greased greaseproof paper in a baking tin
with low sides and sprinkle with crumbs.
Put the mixture on this and spread out to
12 x 16 inches and bake for 15-20 minutes
at 375°F (190°C/Gas Mark 5).
 Mix the sour cream with the mushrooms, heat carefully and spread over the
spinach mixture and roll up like a jam roll,
lifting the paper to help it. *Do not try to roll
up without paper.* Put the roll on a hot
plate and pour the melted margarine over
it, sprinkle with cheese and serve at once.

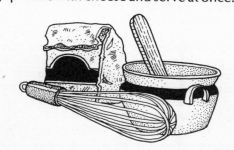

## SPINACH CHEESE BALLS

½ cupful minced raw spinach
½ cupful cottage cheese
Pinch of nutmeg
1½ teaspoonsful grated orange peel
1 large egg
2 tablespoonsful flour
Salted water
Melted margarine
Cheese
Salt and pepper

Press the minced spinach to release the
juice. Put the cottage cheese in the
blender to make it quite smooth then mix
with the spinach and add the seasonings,
orange rind, egg and flour and 1
tablespoonful of cheese. Mix well and roll
into twenty balls. Use as little flour as
possible to make the mixture. Poach the
balls in boiling salted water for not more
than 3 minutes. Lift out with a slotted
spoon. Serve with melted butter and
grated cheese.

## SPINACH PIE
## AU GRATIN

½ lb (225g) short pastry
2½ cupsful cold cooked spinach, chopped
¼ pt. (150ml) thick cream
2 tablespoonsful soft nutter or margarine
½ cupful diced Gouda cheese
Salt and pepper
¼ lb (100g) sliced Gouda cheese

Line a large flan tin with the pastry and
bake it blind filled with greaseproof paper
and baking beans or crusts. Mix the
spinach, cream, nutter or margarine, and
diced cheese and season with salt and
pepper then put in the baked flan shell.
Cover the filling with sliced Gouda cheese
and put into the oven to finish it at 400°F
(200°C/Gas Mark 6). Cook until the
cheese melts.

## SPINACH IN MADEIRA AND CREAM

3 lb (1½kg) spinach
4 tablespoonful Madeira
1 pt. (550ml) thick cream
Salt and black pepper

Wash the spinach in the usual way and cook it in only the water that clings to the leaves. Then drain all liquid from the pan and cook the spinach uncovered to reduce the rest of the water. There should be no water left in the pan. Add the Madeira. Put the cream in a small pan and cook until it is reduced by half; stir into the spinach, season with salt and pepper and serve at once. This is an extravagant recipe but a cheaper version may be made if a smooth, rich white sauce is used instead of the cream: beat a raw egg in at the last minute.

## MASHED SWEET POTATOES

¼ cupful thin cream
2 tablespoonsful nutter
4-5 boiled and then skinned sweet potatoes
Salt and pepper
1 dessertspoonful grated lemon rind (optional)
Juice of 1 lemon (optional)

Heat the cream with the nutter, salt and pepper then mash with the sweet potatoes until light and fluffy. Pile in a dish and serve at once. Use a rotary beater, not an electric one, for this vegetable. In an electric beater they get cold and have to be reheated in the oven and then they lose the creamy texture that is so distinctive. Instead of adding the optional lemon flavouring, try brown sugar or honey or 3 tablespoonsful of sherry and some orange juice and rind. The latter makes an excellent party dish.

## SWEET POTATOES AND PIMIENTOS

Use the recipe for Mashed Sweet Potatoes (above).

1 tin of pimientos
Sprigs of parsley

Grease individual moulds and line each one with a whole pimiento. Then, very carefully, fill the pimientos with the mashed sweet potato mixture. Put each little mould in a deep tin and heat at 350°F (175°C/Gas Mark 4) for 15 minutes. Then turn out the moulds and stick a sprig of parsley in the top of each one.

## SWEET POTATOES AND CHESTNUTS

Recipe for mashed sweet potatoes
1 small jar chestnuts in syrup
2 tablespoonsful rum

Use the recipe omitting the honey and sweeten with the syrup from the chestnuts. Pile in a greased baking dish and cover with chestnuts. Put in the oven at 325°F (160°C/Gas Mark 3) until heated through. Heat the rum, bring it to the table with the dish, pour it over and *flambée* it.

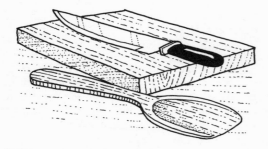

## TOMATO EGGS

Large whole tomatoes, skinned
Brown bread crumbs, mixed with melted nutter or oil
1 egg for each tomato
Cream
Grated Cheese
Toasted bread
Sugar
Salt and pepper

Cut holes in the tops or bottoms of the tomatoes and scoop out most of the insides. Put 1 tablespoonful of crumbs (or bran buds) in each tomato; then drop in a raw egg and a little cream and fill with grated cheese. Sprinkle with salt and pepper. Put the tomatoes close together in a greased baking dish and bake at 350°F (175°C/Gas Mark 4) for 15-20 minutes. If the tomatoes are very ripe, do not skin them or they will burst.

## TOMATO SOUFFLÉ

½ pt. (275ml) tomato *purée*
Grated rind of 1 orange
1 tablespoonful grated mild onion
1½ tablespoonsful nutter or margarine
Salt and pepper
½ pt. (275ml) orange juice
3 oz. (75g) wholemeal flour or 81 per cent flour
4 eggs, separated

Melt the fat and *sauté* the onion in it until tender. Add the *purée*, salt, pepper and orange rind and cook gently for 5 minutes. Mix the orange juice with the flour, add the beaten egg yolks and mix well. Whip the egg whites until stiff and fold into the first mixture. Pour into a baking dish and bake for 25 minutes at 350°F (175°C/Gas Mark 4). Serve a cream sauce separately.

## CREOLE TOMATOES

6 very large ripe tomatoes, skinned and sliced
    across in ½-inch slices
2 tablespoonsful nutter or oil
1 large minced green pepper
2 oz. (50g) minced spring onions or leeks
½ cupful dark treacle
Flour
Sea salt and pepper

Grease a casserole and put in a layer of
tomatoes, then green pepper and onion
and repeat until all are used. Put the
seasoning and a little flour on each layer,
also dot with fat or sprinkle with oil. Pour
the treacle over the top and bake at 300°F
(145°C/Gas Mark 2) for one hour.

## CURRIED TOMATOES
## WITH HERBS

1 large tomato per person
Salt and pepper
Dried fennel, tarragon, basil, rosemary,
    summer savoury, thyme
Nutter

**Curry Sauce**
1½ tablespoonsful oil, nutter or cooking fat
1 tablespoonful curry powder
2 tablespoonsful grated onion
1 cupful orange juice
2½ teaspoonsful cornflour
1 teaspoonful grated orange rind
1 teaspoonful honey

Put the sliced tomatoes in a greased or
oiled baking dish and sprinkle with salt,
pepper and all or some of the herbs. To
make the sauce, put the curry powder and
fat in the top of a double saucepan and
cook over boiling water for 8 minutes.
Then add the onion and cook for a further
3 minutes. Blend the cornflour with the
orange juice and add all the rest of the
ingredients. Cook over low heat in the
double saucepan until thickened. If liked,
2 tablespoonsful of soured cream may be
added. Put the dish of tomatoes in the
oven, a very hot one (450°F (230°C/Gas
Mark 9) and bake for 7-8 minutes.
Remove from the oven and pour the
sauce over them. The tomatoes may be
grilled under high heat in order to save
electricity. Garnish to taste.

## GREEN TOMATOES IN
## SOUR CREAM

6 large green tomatoes, just tinged with red
2 tablespoonsful brown sugar
½ cupful tomato juice
½ cupful sour cream
Salt and pepper

Do not try to use the tiny green tomatoes
for this, they will not do. Remove a small
slice from one end of each tomato then
cut them in halves crosswise. Put them in a
pan with a very little water, sprinkle with
the sugar and add the other ingredients
except the cream. Put in a pan and simmer
for 40 minutes so that the juice reduces a
little. Just heat the soured cream and pour
over the tomatoes.

Buttered Broad Beans
Aubergine Baked With Herbs
Onion Pie

## TOMATO DUMPLINGS

8 oz. (225g) short pastry
6 ripe tomatoes
3 oz. (75g) brown sugar
Salt and pepper

Make any of the vegetarian pastries. Roll out and cut into 6 rounds large enough to enclose a tomato in each. Skin the tomatoes, open them a little at the stem end and put a little sugar, pepper and salt in each one then sprinkle a little of the same mixture on each piece of pastry. Put a tomato on each round of pastry, dampen the edges and bring the pastry up to cover the tomatoes. Put the dumplings, cut side down on a greased baking dish or tin; brush each one with a little milk and bake at 400°F (200°C/Gas Mark 6) for about 30 minutes.

## BAKED TOMATOES STUFFED WITH RICE

6 medium-sized ripe tomatoes
1 cupful cooked brown rice flavoured lightly
    with curry powder
1 teaspoonful grated onion
Nuttered breadcrumbs

Cut a thin slice from the stem ends of the tomatoes and remove the pulp with a small teaspoon and mix with the flavoured rice. Add a few spoonsful of onion then stuff the tomatoes with the mixture. Arrange the tomatoes in a greased baking dish, sprinkle with oiled crumbs and bake at 400°F (200°C/Gas Mark 6) for about 25 to 30 minutes.

These tomatoes are delicious served on a bed of chopped cooked spinach.

## TOMATO PIE NICOISE

8 oz. (225g) flaky pastry
6 tablespoonsful nuttered crumbs
1 cupful cooked green peas
Some firm green or red tomatoes
Black pepper
3 tablespoonsful chopped chives
3 tablespoonsful chopped parsley
1 tablespoonful nutter or margarine
1 tablespoonful olive oil
1 clove of garlic, minced
12 black olives

Line a plate with half the pastry and cover with a layer of the breadcrumbs, about $\frac{1}{2}$ cupful, then put a layer of very thinly sliced tomatoes, sprinkle with salt, black pepper, parsley and chives. Sprinkle with oil or dot with margarine. Sprinkle with garlic and add the onions cut in rings. Put the rest of the tomatoes on top, sprinkle with black pepper and some oil and on top put a layer of black olives sliced and cover with the rest of the pastry. Flatten the rim and trim neatly to seal it. Cut a few slashes in the top and bake at 450°F (230°C/Gas Mark 8) for 10 minutes, then lower the heat to 375°F (190°C/Gas Mark 5) and cook for a further 20 minutes until the pastry is a delicate brown.

A nice additional touch is to pour through an opening in the pastry 2 tablespoonsful of tomato juice mixed with the same amount of sherry.

# ROSE TURNIPS

2½ cupsful peeled, sliced baby turnips
¼ pt. (150ml) soured cream
3 tablespoonsful margarine or nutter
4 tablespoonsful sweet white wine
2½ tablespoonsful paprika
Salt and cayenne pepper

Peel and slice the turnips and put them into a casserole. Mix 1½ tablespoonsful of the paprika with the wine and pour over the vegetable. Sprinkle with pepper and salt and dot with margarine. Bake the casserole at 350°F (175°C/Gas Mark 4), covered for 20-30 minutes, or until the turnips are tender but not mushy. There should not be more than ¼ cupful of liquid left in the casserole; if more, mix the rest of the paprika into the sour cream, put over the turnips and serve hot.

# INDIAN VEGETABLE CURRY

2 oz. (50g) vegetable fat
2 crushed garlic cloves
1 very large onion, grated
1 tablespoonful turmeric
1 tablespoonful coriander
1 teaspoonful crushed cardamon
1 teaspoonful ground ginger
¼ teaspoonful chilli powder
1 teaspoonful cumin powder
1 teaspoonful caraway powder
½ teaspoonful ground cloves
3 tablespoonsful currants
½ teaspoonful dry mustard
1 tablespoonful clear honey
3 tablespoonsful chutney
Salt
½ cupful desiccated coconut
1 cupful strong vegetable stock
½ cupful tomato juice
2 tablespoonsful lemon or lime juice

**Cooked Vegetables**
Steamed cauliflower
Grilled tomatoes
Steamed parsnips
Steamed little onions
Hot boiled rice and Indian chutney

Melt the vegetable fat in the top of a double saucepan, add the garlic and onions then add all the dry ingredients and leave to cook over simmering water for 10 minutes, then add the rest of the sauce ingredients. Stir well, cover and leave to cook at the same heat for 45 minutes. If the list of ingredients terrifies you you may use 3 tablespoonsful of commercial curry powder, but it is more satisfying to make your own.

Put the hot vegetables in a hot dish and pour the sauce over them. This is not a excessively strong curry sauce and real addicts may add red pepper. Almost any vegetables may be used, either together or separately.

Always use long grain rice and cook it with the greatest care and rinse well. Remember to have little dishes of nuts, plenty of sweet mango chutney and coconut to go with the curry.

## BAKED MIXED VEGETABLES WITH RICE

1 measuring cupful brown rice
½ cupful each of diced carrots, turnips and
    shredded cabbage
2 potatoes, peeled and sliced thinly
1 onion, peeled and sliced thinly
1 cupful diced tomatoes
½ teaspoonful each of chopped parsley and
    dried basil
2 pt. (1¼l) strong vegetable stock

Grease a baking dish and put the rice in it, add the carrots, turnips and cabbage, then a layer of potatoes, then onions, then tomatoes and herbs, with salt and pepper to taste. Pour the stock on top, cover the dish and bake for 3 hours at 325°F (160°C/Gas Mark 3) or until the vegetables are tender.

## VEGETABLE STEW WITH PINWHEEL TOP

2 tablespoonful nutter or margarine
4 tablespoonsful 81 per cent flour
1 pt. (550ml) milk
1 bay leaf
2 cloves
Salt and pepper
1 teaspoonful curry powder mixed with the
    same amount of milk
16 pickling onions, boiled
1 cupful cooked green peas
1 cupful cooked french beans, chopped
3 cooked carrots, sliced
1 cupful skinned and cooked tomatoes

**Pinwheel Top**
10 oz. (275g) 81 per cent flour
3 teaspoonsful baking powder
½ teaspoonful celery salt
4 tablespoonsful cooking fat
4 oz. (100g) grated sharp cheese
Cold vegetable stock as required to moisten

To make the stew, melt the nutter or margarine and blend in the 4 table-spoonsful of flour, cook until it bubbles then add the milk which has been scalded with the bay leaf and cloves. Stir and cook until thick and smooth, then add the salt, curry powder and a little pepper made to a paste with cold milk. Bring to the boil again and cook for 5 minutes. Add the vegetables, stir and pour into an ovenware dish and cover with the pinwheels.

To make the pinwheel top, sift the flour, baking powder and celery salt in a mixing bowl, cut in the cooking fat, mix and add the grated cheese. Moisten with cold vegetable stock to make a soft dough. Roll the dough out ¼-inch thick, spread with the cheese and roll up like a Swiss roll. Cut into slices and arrange close together on top of the dish of vegetables. Bake at 425°F (215°C/Gas Mark 7) for 20 minutes. Serve at once.

# SAUCES

Here are a few recipes for sauces suitable to be served with various vegetables.

## MUSHROOM SAUCE

3 tablespoonsful chopped onion
1½ cupsful vegetable liquid from whatever
    vegetable has been cooked
2 dessertspoonsful cornflour
Salt and cayenne pepper
Pinch nutmeg
1 cupful mushrooms, *sautéed* or stewed
2 dessertspoonsful margarine

Blend the vegetable liquor with a little cream and mix with the cornflour, then add the other ingredients and cook until it thickens then pour over the chosen vegetable. Garnish with chopped parsley or chives.

## TOMATO SAUCE

3 tablespoonsful chopped onion
3 tablespoonsful chopped green pepper
Vegetable water and tinned tomato juice to
    make ¾ cupful
3 teaspoonsful cornflour
3 tablespoonsful soured cream

Cook the onion in with the vegetable and add the green pepper as soon as the water boils again. When the vegetable is just tender, strain off the liquid and use with the tomato juice. Blend with the cornflour and cook until it thickens, then take off the heat and mix in the soured cream. Pour over the vegetable and scatter bran buds on top.

## LEMON CAPER SAUCE

Vegetable liquor
2 tablespoonsful margarine
1 tablespoonful grated onion or onion salt
Pepper and salt, if just onion is used
1 teaspoonful turmeric
Cornflour
2 tablespoonsful capers

Drain the water from the cooked vegetable, add all the ingredients except the capers and blend in 1 teaspoonful of cornflour to every ¼ pt. (150ml) of liquid. Cook until it thickens then add the capers and pour over the vegetable. Sprinkle parsley on top.

## MUSTARD SAUCE

4 tablespoonsful melted nutter or margarine
Pinch of sugar
1 teaspoonful dry mustard
2 teaspoonsful lemon juice
Salt and pepper
Pinch of nutmeg

Mix all the ingredients in a pan and simmer to thicken, beat with a whisk.

## CAULIFLOWER WITH NUTS

½ lb (225g) cauliflower
4 oz. (100g) nuts, any kind
4 tablespoonsful mayonnaise

Cut the nuts into little pieces about the size of a hazel nut. Shred the well-washed cauliflower and mix both with the mayonnaise.

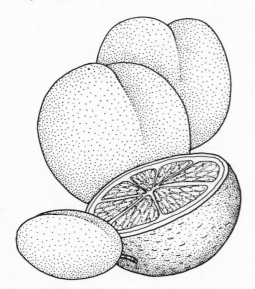

## PANCAKES FILLED WITH NUTS

**Pancake Batter:**
4 oz. (100g) flour
1 egg
Sea salt
½ pt. (275ml) milk (or a little more according to type of flour)

Sift the flour and salt, make a hollow in the middle and drop in the egg and half the milk. Beat well and then add the rest of the milk. Fry in a small oiled frying pan. The mixture will make eight pancakes. Keep the pancakes hot on greaseproof paper, fill and roll when all are cooked.

**Stuffing:**
2 oz. (50g) grated nuts
2 large tomatoes
½ pt. (275ml) white sauce
2 tablespoonsful oil
3 tablespoonsful breadcrumbs
½ teaspoonful garlic or onion salt
Pinch of sea salt

Heat the oil and fry the chopped, skinned tomatoes in it with the onion or garlic salt and a pinch of sea salt. Cook gently for about 5 minutes. Mix in the breadcrumbs and nuts. Cook just enough to heat through then mix in the sauce and fill the pancakes with the mixture. Serve very hot. Grated cheese may be handed or sprinkled on top of the rolled pancakes.

## NUT CUTLET

2 oz. (50g) grated nuts
4 oz. (100g) fine breadcrumbs
2 oz. (50g) vegetarian fat
2 oz. (50g) brown flour
Salt to taste
1 raw egg
1 pt. (550ml) vegetable stock
1 teaspoonful Marmite
2 tablespoonsful milk
Any herbs to taste
Oil for frying

Melt the fat in a pan, add the flour and stir and cook for not less than 2 minutes. Warm the stock and add it and the salt, herbs and Marmite. Cook and stir for 5 minutes; taste, and if the taste is 'raw' continue to cook for a few more minutes. Take off the heat and add 3 oz. (75g) of the breadcrumbs and the nuts. Leave on a plate or dish to cool then form into cutlets. Mix the egg and milk, dip the cutlets in it and then in the reserved breadcrumbs. Fry in oil until golden brown.

## NUT RISSOLES

2 oz. (50g) red lentils
2 oz. (50g) minced nuts
3 breakfast cupsful breadcrumbs
2 eggs
Marjoram and thyme to taste
Salt
2 tablespoonsful milk
Oil for frying

Soak the lentils overnight in 1 quart (1¼l) of water then cook in the same water until soft. Mix the drained lentils with the nuts, 2 cupsful of the breadcrumbs, 1 egg, salt and herbs and leave to stand for 30 minutes. Then form into rissoles. Beat the egg and milk together and coat the rissoles with the mixture and dip in the breadcrumbs. Leave for a few minutes to dry and then fry in deep fat until browned.

## NUT ROAST

½ lb (225g) tomatoes
½ lb (225g) grated walnuts
2 shallots
1 teaspoonful oil
2 eggs
1 teaspoonful chopped parsley and chives
Salt to taste

Peel the tomatoes and slice them. Skin and chop the shallots. Mix the nuts and tomatoes and shallots together and blend with the well-beaten eggs, add salt and herbs. Grease a fireproof dish or bread tin, put the mixture in it and bake in the oven preheated to 400°F (200°C/Gas Mark 7) for 30-40 minutes. It should be well-risen and golden brown when done. Serve hot, turned out and with any sauce liked.

## SPINACH WITH NUTS

½ lb (225g) spinach
3 teaspoonsful lemon juice
2 level teaspoonsful sugar
5 oz. (150g) grated nuts
4 tablespoonsful mayonnaise

Wash the spinach well and choose young leaves, shake it in a salad drier to get rid of as much water as possible. Chop it very finely (do not use any of the stems). Now mix with all the other ingredients, adding the mayonnaise last. Pile in a dish and serve nice and cold.

## NUT SAUCE

¼ lb (100g) nuts, any mixture
1½ cupsful mayonnaise
1 teaspoonful brown sugar
2 teaspoonsful lemon juice

Put the nuts on a baking sheet and heat the oven to 300°F (150°C/Gas Mark 2) for about 20 minutes or until they are crisp. Rub on a towel to get rid of as much brown skin as possible. Put through the liquidizer and then mix with the lemon juice and sugar, lastly fold in the mayonnaise.

# Chapter Four
# PUDDINGS

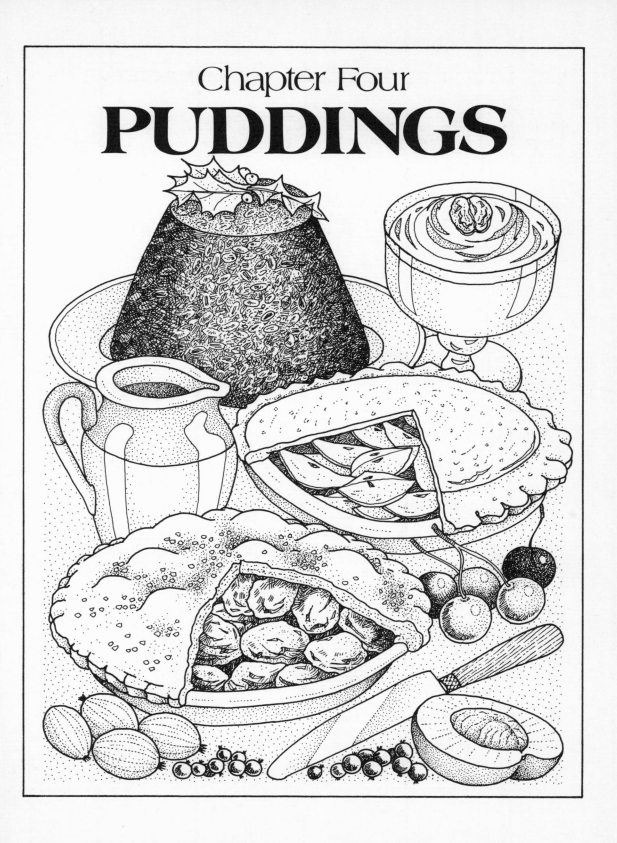

For genuine 'vegetarian' puddings and desserts remember to use vegetable fats, brown sugar and either wholemeal of 81 per cent flour, gelozone instead of gelatine, brown rice, free-range eggs and no suet. There is a substitute for suet in Suenut.

# AMBROSIA

2 oz. (50g) rolled oats
1 cupful cornflakes
½ oz. (15g) grated walnuts
1½ oz. (40g) nuts, chopped or grated
½ pt. (275ml) thin cream
1 oz. (25g) butter or margarine
2 oz. (50g) brown sugar or honey
1½ oz. (40g) sultanas or raisins

Melt the fat in a strong frying pan, add the oats and ½ oz. (15g) of nuts and cook over low heat until lightly brown. Stir from time to time or they will burn. Add the sugar or honey and cook for 3-5 minutes stirring all the time. Now turn into a mixing bowl, add the cornflakes, the rest of the nuts and the sultanas or raisins. Mix well and serve cold with the cream.

# APPLE TART

**Pastry**
3 oz. (75g) margarine or cooking fat
6 oz. (175g) flour
3 oz. (75g) sugar
1 egg
1 tablespoonful milk

**Filling**
¾ lb (325g) cooking apples
1 tablespoonful cake or bread crumbs
4 oz. (100g) brown sugar
1 oz. (25g) sultanas

To make the pastry, sift the flour, and add the sugar and rub in the fat until fine. Beat the egg slightly and add (but reserve a little for the top of the tart). Make a paste with the milk and add a pinch of salt. Mix to a ball and leave to stand for 30 minutes. Then cut the pastry in half and roll out one piece to a round and line a sandwich tin 8 inches in diameter with it. Fill with a piece of paper and baking beans or crusts and bake for 15 minutes at 400°F (200°C/Gas Mark 6). Then make the filling. Peel and core the apples and cut them into neat slices. Take the baked pastry shell and put in it a layer of cake or bread crumbs, then the sliced apples then the sultanas and lastly the sugar. Roll out the other piece of pastry, dampen the edge of the lower pastry and cover it with the top layer and press on the rim to seal. Trim neatly and mark the rim with the prongs of a fork. Paint the top with the reserved egg and sprinkle a little sugar on it. Bake for 30-40 minutes at the same temperature. This is just as good hot as it is cold.

## APPLE PUDDING

1 lb (450g) cooking apples
4 cloves
2 tablespoonsful seedless raisins
1 tablespoonful lemon juice
2 tablespoonsful sugar

**Batter**
2 cupsful 81 per cent flour
pinch of salt
½ cupful brown sugar
2 eggs
1 pt. (550ml) milk

Peel, slice and core the apples and cover the bottom of a fireproof dish with them. Add the cloves and raisins, sprinkle with lemon juice and sugar. Make a batter from the ingredients given then pour over the apples. Bake at 350°F (175°C/Gas Mark 4) for 1 hour.

## APPLES BAKED WITH GERANIUM LEAVES

4 green cooking apples
1 tablespoonful apple jelly
4 apple-scented geranium leaves
A little butter or nutter

Cut a little from the tops of the apples and remove the cores. Put a little fat on the hollows and put a teaspoonful of apple jelly in each apple and top with a scented geranium leaf. Stand the apples in a little water in a fireproof dish. Put the apples in and bake at 350°F (175°C/Gas Mark 4) until soft, time cannot be given for this because apples vary so much. When the apples are soft, pour the juice from the dish into a saucepan, add a tablespoonful of sugar and boil for a few minutes, then add a drop or two of red colouring and pour this syrup over the apples. Eat hot. The geranium leaves may also be eaten.

## BALM AND MARSHMALLOW CUSTARD

6 marshmallows
2 eggs
1½ tablespoonsful sugar
1 pt. (550ml) milk
1 tablespoonful fresh lemon balm leaves
1 vanilla pod

Cut the marshmallows in half cross-wise and put them in the bottom of a well-greased, fire-proof dish. Whisk the eggs and sugar together then add the milk, beat well and pour over the marshmallows. Put the vanilla pod into the custard and sprinkle the balm leaves on top. Put the dish in a tin of water and bake at 300°F (145°C/Gas Mark 2) until the custard is set.

## BAKED PEARS AND CARDAMON

Peel, slice and core some pears and put them in a shallow ovenproof dish, sprinkle with sugar and add to 4-5 pears. Add a tablespoonful of wine or liqueur. Sprinkle with a teaspoonful of cracked cardamon seeds (crack them with a rolling pin). Bake at 350°F (175°C/Gas Mark 4) until the pears are soft. Leave to cool. A little cream may be served with this delicately flavoured dish. It is a splendid way of cooking rather tasteless pears.

## BILBERRY TART

½ lb (225g) rich short pastry
1 lb (450g) bilberries
5 oz. (150g) sugar
¼ teaspoonful cinnamon

Roll half the pastry out and line an 8-inch pie plate with it. Spread the bilberries over it mixed with the sugar and cinnamon. Roll out the rest of the pastry and cover the filling after damping the rim. Seal carefully and press down with the prongs of a fork or the end of a spoon. Trim neatly. Slash the top on a few places and sprinkle with sugar if liked. Bake at 400°F (200°C/Gas Mark 6) for 25-30 minutes. Custard or cream go well with this tart.

## CHRISTMAS PUDDING

10 oz. (275g) mixed dried fruit
1 teaspoonful mixed spice
¼ teaspoonful ground ginger
¼ teaspoonful grated nutmeg
2 oz. (50g) sugar
1 tablespoonful chocolate powder
¾ pt. (425ml) water
8 tablespoonsful bottled orange juice
¼ oz. (7g) gelozone
3 oz. (75g) chopped cut peel
1 tablespoonful sherry
Double cream (optional)

Put the fruit, spices, chocolate powder and sugar into a pan, add the water and orange juice and boil for 5 minutes. Take off the heat and add the gelozone mixed with a little warm water to soften it. Add the sherry and peel and mix well. Rinse a 7½-inch ring mould with water and then put the mixture into it and leave in a cold place to set. Turn out to serve. The centre may be filled with whipped cream and rosettes of piped cream when it is wanted for a party.

## CRANBERRY GRAPE SALAD

1 lb (450g) cranberries
9 oz. (250g) sugar
¾ lb (325g) grapes, halved and de-pipped
1 cupful sliced celery
4 oz. (100g) chopped nuts
12 marshmallows, halved
½ pt. (275ml) whipped cream

Mince the cranberries and mix the sugar with them; a fine blade should be used for the mincing. Add the rest of the fruit and the celery, chopped finely. Whip the cream and fold it in. Serve in little glass bowls individually.

## CORIANDER APPLE CRUMBLE

3-4 apples
1 tablespoonful brown sugar
1 teaspoonful cinnamon
1 cupful plain flour
½ cupful brown sugar
4 oz. (100g) nutter or margarine
1 teaspoonful crushed coriander seeds

Slice the peeled, cored apples and cover the bottom of a fireproof dish with them. Sprinkle with the brown sugar and cinnamon. Rub the fat into the flour and add the sugar and press on top of the apples. Then sprinkle with the crushed coriander seed. Bake at 350°F (175°C/Gas Mark 4) for about half an hour.

## STEAMED DATE PUDDING

½ lb (225g) stoned dates
2 oz. (50g) self-raising flour
2 oz. (50g) soft breadcrumbs
2 oz. (50g) light brown sugar
3 oz. (75g) Suenut
Good pinch of salt
¼ teaspoonful ground ginger
¼ teaspoonful ground cinnamon
1 tablespoonful sherry
2 tablespoonsful milk
1 egg

Chop the dates into fairly small pieces. Mix all the dry ingredients together. Beat the sherry and milk with the egg (the sherry may be omitted if not liked). Mix with the dry ingredients. Grease a 2 pt. (1¼ l) pudding basin and put the mixture into it. Cover with cooking foil and steam for 2½ hours. Serve with golden syrup, custard or cream.

91

## DATE AND ORANGE FLAN

8 oz. (225g) stoned dates
4 tablespoonsful stout
¼ teaspoonful ground cardamon
¼ teaspoonful ground cinnamon
2 Jaffa oranges
Baked pie shell of short pastry (7 inch)

Chop the dates and cook them in the stout and spices until the mixture is like thick jam. It will take about 7 minutes.

Grate the rind of one of the oranges and peel the other one. Cut both in thin slices then remove the pith with scissors. Spread the date mixture in the pastry case and arrange the slices in a circle round the top and pour the syrup on top and leave to set.

## FRUIT CREAM

1 small eating apple
1 pear
5 cherries
½ orange
A few grapes
4 oz. (100g) lemon curd
4 oz. (100g) cottage cheese
2 tablespoonsful sugar
1 tablespoonful lemon juice
1 tablespoonful grated nuts

Mix the cheese, lemon juice and milk to a smooth cream then add the sugar. Chop the fruit into very small pieces with the other ingredients and serve in glass dishes sprinkled with the nuts. Serves four.

## FRUIT MEDLEY

6 oz. (175g) dried fruit, prunes, dates, apricots, etc
1 oz. (25g) sultanas or raisins
1 small red apple
1 oz. (25g) desiccated coconut
2 tablespoonsful
2 tablespoonsful grated nuts

Put the dried fruit and apple through a mincer then add the grated nuts. Grease a baking sheet with oil and spread the mixture on it, not too thinly. Press down and sprinkle with coconut. Leave to stand for 3 hours, then cut into pieces; squares or oblongs and serve with cream.

## FILLED APRICOTS

2 fresh apricots
1 tablespoonful whipped cream
1 heaped teaspoonful grated nuts
1 teaspoonful vanilla sugar
A little grated chocolate (optional)

Cut the apricots in halves and remove the stones. Mix the other ingredients together and fill the hollows in the fruit.

## FRUIT TRIFLE

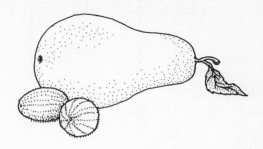

1½ cupsful cornflakes
2 tablespoonsful milk with 2 tablespoonsful
    brown sugar
2 medium-sized eating apples
2 tablespoonsful milk
2 bananas
A few black or green grapes
½ pt. (275ml) whipping cream

Crush the cornflakes, mix them with the sugar and line the bottom of a dish with them. Grate the apples, mash the bananas and mix with the milk; then spread on top of the cornflakes. Cover with a thick layer of whipped cream and decorate with de-pipped grapes. Chill for 2 hours in the refrigerator.

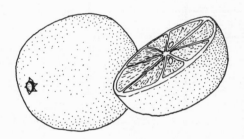

## FRESH FRUIT SALD WITH CRANBERRY DRESSING

2-3 ripe peaches
3 ripe bananas
1 large fresh pineapple or a large tin of sliced
    pineapple
2 teaspoonsful sugar
Juice of ½ orange
Juice of ½ lemon
¼ pt. (150ml) jellied cranberry sauce
4 tablespoonsful mayonnaise

Make the salad with the fruits as usual. For the dressing, blend together the mayonnaise, cranberry sauce, lemon and orange juice and sugar. Serve separately. Serves from 6-8.

## FRUIT SALAD WITH PECAN DRESSING

2 red skinned apples, cored and diced
2 pears, peeled, cored and diced
½ lb (225g) seeded grapes
3 ripe bananas, sliced
1 cupful tinned pineapple, cubed
1 oz. (25g) shelled pecans, toasted and
    chopped
1 teaspoonful sugar
1 tablespoonful lemon juice
¼ pt. (275ml) orange juice
½ pt. (275ml) whipped cream

Whip the cream and whip in the orange and lemon juices and fold in the pecans. To prepare the pecans, toast them at 350°F (175°C/Gas Mark 4) for 10 minutes – it enchances their flavour. Mix together all the prepared fruits and fold into the dressing. Serves 8.

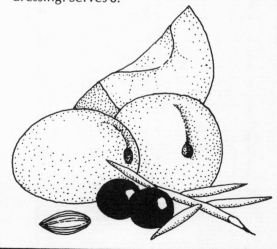

93

## GLAZED PEARS

4 large ripe pears
1 cupful passion fruit pulp or blackcurrant
   *purée*
1 cup ful water
½ cupful sugar
A few pieces of angelica
1 teaspoonful cinnamon or 4 crushed
   coriander seeds
A little nutter or margarine

Wipe the pears and core them from the stem end. In each one put a knob of margarine or nutter, 1 crushed coriander seed and some sugar. Make a syrup from the ½ cupful sugar and 1 cupful of water boiled together for 10 minutes. Put the pears in a saucepan and pour the syrup over them. Cover the pan and simmer gently until just tender, spooning the syrup over them frequently, then add the chosen *purée*. Lift the pears out very carefully on to a dish then pour the mixed *purée* and syrup over them. Give each pear an angelica stalk. Chill and serve with thick cream.

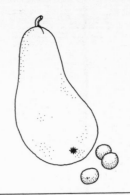

## LEMON SCENTED BAKED CUSTARD

3 eggs
1 pt. (550ml) milk
2 tablespoonsful light brown sugar
1 medium-sized, lemon-scented geranium leaf
A little margarine or nutter

Break the eggs into an ovenware dish, add the sugar and beat with a fork; pour the milk over gradually as you beat. Dot with fat and place the geranium leaf on top. Put the dish in a tin of water and bake at 350°F (175C/Gas Mark 4) for about ¾ hour. You may use a geranium leaf this way with rice pudding.

## GINGER SPONGE PUDDING

3 oz. (75g) margarine
2 oz. (50g) sugar (dark brown)
1 egg
1½ tablespoonsful golden syrup or treacle
5 oz. (150g) self-raising 81 per cent flour
2 teaspoonsful ground ginger
1 teaspoonful mixed spice
Good pinch of salt
Warm syrup as sauce

Cream the butter and sugar, beat in the egg, syrup and lastly the flour sifted with the ginger, mixed spice and salt. Grease a 2pt. (1¼l) pudding basin, put in mixture, cover tightly with cooking foil and steam for 1¾ hours. Serve the warmed syrup over the pudding, diluting it a little with lemon if you like.

## LEMON SOUFFLÉ WITH LEMON SAUCE

**Soufflé**

1½ oz. (40g) margarine
1½ oz. (40g) flour
6 tablespoonsful milk
4 eggs
3 oz. (75g) sugar
Rind 1 lemon

Melt the margarine in a saucepan and stir in the flour. Mix well and then add the milk, stir and cook for 5 minutes. Let it cool a little then beat in the sugar and grated lemon rind. Separate the eggs and beat in the yolks one at a time. Whisk the egg whites until a stiff peak forms when the beater is lifted; then fold into the first mixture with a metal spoon. Pour into a casserole or *soufflé* dish, prepared with a paper collar, but only half fill the dish because this *soufflé* rises to twice the original quantity. Bake for 30 minutes at 375°F (190°C/Gas Mark 5). Serve at once.

**Sauce**

1½ cupsful water
1½ lemons
2 oz. (50g) sugar
2 teaspoonsful cornflour

Grate the rind from the lemons and squeeze out the juice. Mix all the ingredients together, except the cornflour. Heat in a saucepan, mix the cornflour with a little cold water then add to the boiling mixture. Cook and stir over a low heat for 6-8 minutes. Serve hot with the *soufflé*.

## MANGO MOUSSE

2 large ripe mangoes or a 1 lb (450g) tin
1 teaspoonful ground ginger
½ pt. (275ml) water
4 oz. (100g) sugar
1 envelope of gelozone dissolved in ¼ cupful hot water
2 eggs, separated
½ pt. (275ml) cream, whipped

Simmer the water, sugar and ginger together for a few minutes. If tinned mangoes are used, the syrup from the tin can replace some of the water. Peel and slice the raw mangoes and poach in the syrup until tender; then sieve them or put through a blender. Add the dissolved gelozone and return to the saucepan with the egg yolks beaten in. Stir over very low heat until smooth and thickened, but *do not boil*. Remove from the heat, cool slightly and fold in the whipped cream and the stiffly beaten egg whites, then pour into a bowl or individual dishes and chill in the refrigerator. Just before serving, sprinkle the tops with toasted shredded coconut which gives a delightful crispness in contrast to the bland mousse. If even tinned mangoes are unobtainable, a 1 lb (450g) tin of peaches may be used.

## MARSHMALLOW AND MINT CUSTARD

Beat three eggs with a fork in an ovenware dish and add 1 tablespoonful of sugar. Slowly add 1pt. (550ml) of milk. Chop enough mint to make 3 teaspoonsful or use 2 teaspoonsful of dried mint. Then float about 24 marshmallows on top. Stand the dish in a tin of water and cook at 350°F (175°C/Gas Mark 4) until set, about 30 minutes.

## PAIN SUCRÉ

3 lightly-beaten egg yolks
6 tablespoonsful milk
1 teaspoonful vanilla extract
Margarine
2 tablespoonsful sugar
Pinch of salt
6 slices of bread
Castor sugar

Remove the crusts from the bread (large tin loaves are the right size for this pudding). Add the vanilla and sugar to the milk. Dip the bread slices in the milk but do this quickly or the bread will either break or be too soggy. Add the salt to the beaten egg yolks and drip the slices in the mixture. Heat the margarine and fry the slices in it. Sprinkle with sugar and serve at once.

## ORANGE DELISH

White of 4 eggs
4 tablespoonsful marmalade
3-4 tablespoonsful sugar
4 large oranges

Beat the egg whites until stiff but not dry. Beat in the marmalade and sugar. Grease the top and sides of a double saucepan, pour in the mixture and cover it. Put over boiling water. Cook for 50 minutes without removing the cover. Turn out and fill oranges, cool and serve with whipped cream. Looks very pretty decorated with tinned orange or mandarin slices.

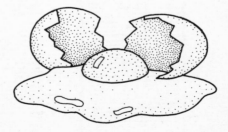

Ginger Biscuits
Banana Bread
Herb Scones
Rice Cake
Walnut Macaroons

## PRUNE WHIP

3 egg whites
1 lb (450g) prunes, cooked and stoned
2 tablespoonsful lemon juice
½ cupful sugar
1 teaspoonful grated lemon rind
Good pinch of salt

Put all the ingredients in a deep bowl and beat with an electric whisk until the mixture will hold its shape. Then chill and serve with cream or custard made from the egg yolks and milk.

## PANCAKES

1 large or 2 small eggs
4 oz. (100g) and 3 teaspoonsful plain flour
Pinch of salt
½ pt. (275ml) milk

Sieve the flour and salt into a basin; make a well in the centre and drop in the egg or eggs, then mix and add the milk slowly and stir until the batter is like thin cream. Do not beat because this makes the batter tough. Put aside for about 10 minutes, stir once and put into a jug. Just before using, add 1 tablespoonful of oil to the batter and stir, then there will be no need to keep greasing the pan. Use a pan about 6-7 inches in diameter. There are all kinds of fillings to be used in pancakes, such as plumped sultanas in a little cream or jam or stewed fruit. But do not fill the pancakes if they are to be stored.

## RUSSIAN CREAM

½ pt. (275ml) milk
6 oz. (175g) curd cheese or cream cheese
1 teaspoonful lemon juice
2 oz. (50g) sugar
2 oz. (50g) sultanas and raisins, mixed
2 oz. (50g) grated nuts

Beat the cheese and milk to a thick cream, add the rest of the ingredients and mix well.

## RHUBARB SLICES

4 slices wholemeal bread
¾ lb (325g) rhubarb
1 oz. (25g) margarine or butter
4 oz. (100g) sugar
3 tablespoonsful cream

Trim the rhubarb and wipe it, do not peel it, then cut it into 1-inch pieces and put with the sugar (but no water) into a pan and stew over very low heat. The fruit should be soft after 10 minutes; do not cook until it falls to pieces. Melt the fat in a frying pan and fry the bread slices in it then arrange the rhubarb on the bread. Whip the cream and decorate the slices with it. Serve hot or cold.

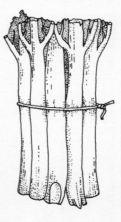

Orange and Onion Salad

## RHUBARB WITH ANGELICA LEAVES

4-5 sticks rhubarb
4 young angelica leaves
½ pt. (275ml) water
4 oz. (100g) sugar
2 thin curls of lemon peel

Wipe the rhubarb and cut it into pieces, put into a pan with all the other ingredients and simmer until tender. Serve with yogurt.

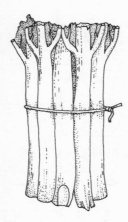

## SAGOU LA PLACE

1½ pt. (825ml) milk
1 vanilla pod
2 oz. (50g) sago
2 oz. (50g) sugar
3 fl.oz. (75ml) double cream
1 egg yolk
4 glacé cherries

Put the milk and vanilla pod in a pan and bring to the boil then scatter in the sago and cook until all is transparent (this will take from 15-20 minutes). Take off the heat and lift out the vanilla pod. Whisk in the sugar and egg yolk. Leave to cool, stirring often to prevent a skin on top then pour into 4 glasses or dishes and chill. Decorate with a cherry or some whipped cream.

## REBANADES

4 thick slices of bread from a large loaf
1 egg
¼ pt. (150ml) milk
1 egg
½ teaspoonful salt
Olive oil
Honey
Cinnamon

Remove the crusts and cut the bread into triangles. Beat the egg and salt and beat into the milk, then soak the bread in this mixture for 1 minutes. Heat a pan of oil to 350°-370·F (180°-185°C/Gas Mark 4). Fry the triangles in the oil until golden on both sides. Drain and serve sprinkled with honey and cinnamon mixed.

## GOOSEBERRY AND SAFFRON SHORTCAKE

8 oz. self-raising 81 per cent flour
$\frac{1}{4}$ teaspoonful powdered saffron
$\frac{1}{4}$ teaspoonful salt
3 oz. (50g) brown sugar
$\frac{1}{4}$ lb. (100g) butter or margarine
1 dessertspoonful arrowroot
1 lb (450g) gooseberries
$\frac{1}{4}$ pint. (150ml) milk
Cream

Sift the flour, saffron and salt into a bowl, add the brown sugar, rub in the fat and add egg and milk. Spoon into a greased 8 inch tin and bake at 400°F (200°C/Gas Mark 6) for 15 minutes. Cool slightly and turn out in to a wire tray. Stew the gooseberries or better still use a 1 lb (450g) tin of gooseberries. Turn the liquid into a pan and simmer to reduce it a little, then thicken it with the arrowroot mixed with a little milk. When thickened, pour over the cake and serve with cream.

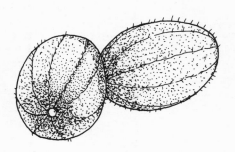

## SPANISH CREAM

3 eggs
$\frac{1}{2}$ cupful sugar
Pinch of salt
$\frac{1}{2}$ teaspoonful almond essence
1 oz. (25g) gelozone
$2\frac{1}{2}$ cupsful milk

Mix the gelozone, sugar and salt with the milk and let them stand for 5 minutes. Put in the top of a double saucepan over simmering water and stir until the gelazone is dissolved. Beat the egg yolks slightly and stir into the hot milk. Cook until the custard will coat the back of a spoon (about 15 minutes). Cool for 10 minutes and add the essence. Beat the egg whites until glossy with folding peaks. Turn the custard into a bowl and fold in the egg whites. Turn into moulds and serve very cold.

## SUPPERTIME GINGER PUDDING

2 eggs
$2\frac{1}{2}$ cups sifted 81 per cent flour
$1\frac{1}{2}$ teaspoonsful baking powder
1 teaspoonful bicarbonate of soda
$\frac{1}{2}$ teaspoonful salt
$1\frac{1}{2}$ teaspoonful cinnamon
1-$1\frac{1}{2}$ teaspoonsful ground ginger
$\frac{1}{4}$ teaspoonful nutmeg
$\frac{1}{2}$ cupful seedless raisins
$\frac{1}{2}$ cupful chopped walnuts
2 tablespoonsful dark treacle
1 cupful dark brown sugar
2 tablespoonsful cooking fat or margarine
1 cupful boiling water

Sift together all the dry ingredients. Mix a cupful of this with the raisins and nuts. Mix the sugar, treacle and eggs and beat well. Then add the fat and the dry ingredients, blend in the hot water and then the floured nuts and raisins. Pour into a greased tin and bake at 350°F (175°C/Gas Mark 4) for 50-60 minutes. Serve hot as a pudding or cold as a cake.

## SWEET APRICOTS

4 oz. (100g) dried apricots
1 tablespoonful clear honey
1 pt. (550ml) milk
1 teaspoonful lemon juice

Wash the apricots and cut them in quarters. Warm the milk enough to dissolve the honey in it, then pour over the apricots and leave to cool. When cold, sprinkle with the lemon juice. Leave to stand for not less than 12 hours.

## YORKSHIRE TREACLE TART

**Pastry**
½ lb (225g) wholemeal flour
1 teaspoonful baking powder
Pinch of salt
3-4 oz. (75-100g) butter or margarine
¾ cupful cold water

**Filling**
3 tablespoonsful golden syrup
1 dessertspoonful lemon juice
1 teaspoonful grated lemon rind
3 heaped tablespoonsful fine soft breadcrumbs
1 teaspoonful cinnamon (optional)

Sift the flour, baking powder and salt and then rub in the fat, add enough cold water to make a firm dough. Roll out on a floured surface. Line a pie plate with the pastry, trim the edges and then fold them in and pinch up in a rim. Prick all over the base. Make the filling by putting the syrup in a pan, using a hot spoon to do this to make the measuring easy. Add the lemon juice, rind and breadcrumbs. Warm slightly over low heat so that all may be mixed, then pour into the pastry lining and sprinkle with cinnamon if used. Bake at 350°F (175°C/Gas Mark 4) for 25-30 minutes. Serve cold or warm, not hot.

## ZABAGLIONE

Yolks of 4 eggs
1½ oz. (40g) sugar
¼ pt. (150ml) Marsala

Put the egg yolks and sugar into a basin and beat until they are a pale primrose colour, add the Marsala and blend. Cook over boiling water in the top of a double saucepan, beating all the time, but make sure the mixture does not boil. When it begins to rise in the pan, take off the fire and serve in glasses. Serve hot or cold. Madeira may be used instead of Marsala.

# Chapter Five
# TEATIME RECIPES

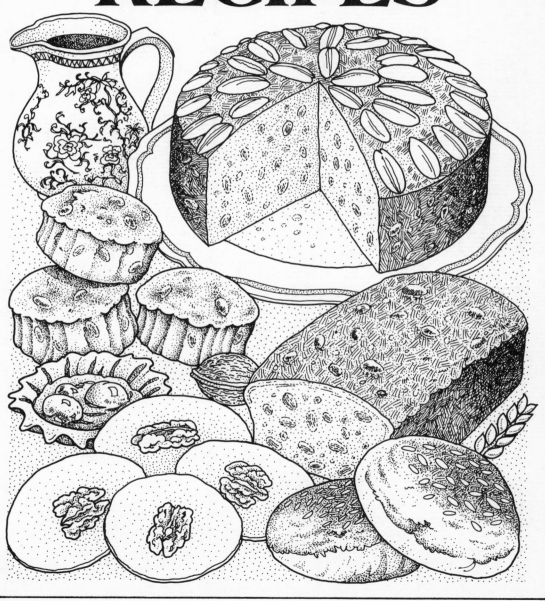

The remarks made in the last chapter about puddings applies to cakes, cookies scones and breads. It is important when cooking for strict vegetarians to use vegetable fats, brown sugar, wholemeal or 81 per cent flour, gelozone or agar-agar instead of gelatine, brown rice instead of white, and free-range eggs.

## ANNE'S ANISEED COOKIES

4 oz. (100g) self raising 81 per cent flour
4 oz. (100g) butter, margarine or nutter
6 oz. (175g) demerara sugar
1 egg
Pinch of salt
1 cupful rolled oats
2 teaspoonsful aniseed
1½ cupsful desiccated coconut

Cream the fat and sugar until pale and thick, add the egg and beat well. Sift the flour and salt and stir it in to the creamed mixture. Mix the oats, coconut and aniseed and add to the mixture and make to a stiff consistency. Roll into small balls and arrange on a greased oven tin and bake at 350°F (175°C/Gas Mark 4) for 12-15 minutes. Cool on the trays and then store.

## BANANA BREAD

10 oz. (275g) self raising 81 per cent flour
½ teaspoonful bicarbonate soda
¼ teaspoonful sea salt
¼ teaspoonful ground cardamon
¼ teaspoonful ground mace
4 oz. (100g) margarine
6 oz. (175g) sugar
2 eggs
¼ teaspoonful vanilla essence
4 oz. (100g) (about 3) bananas
3 oz. (75g) chopped walnuts

Sift the flour, soda, salt and spices several times. Cream the fat and sugar, beat in the eggs and essence then stir in the flour and banana alternately; lastly add the nuts. Grease and flour a bread tin and put the mixture into it, level the top and back at 350°F (175°C/Gas Mark 4) for 60 minutes. Do not turn out of the tin until the loaf is cold. Serve in slices, buttered.

# CHRISTMAS CAKE

7 oz. (200g) plain flour
1 oz. (25g) self-raising flour
½ lb (225g) margarine
3 oz. (75g) demerara sugar
½ cupful clear honey
5 free-range eggs
1 level teaspoonful each of salt, cinnamon,
    ground cloves, allspice and nutmeg
Juice and grated rind of 1 lemon
4 oz. (100g) each of *glacé* cherries, sultanas,
    stoned raisins, crystallized pineapple, *glacé*
    figs, mixed peel, shelled almonds
1 sherry glass of rum or the same amount
    orange juice

Prepare the fruit, halve the cherries and chop the larger fruit into small pieces. Sift the flour, spices and salt together and mix a cupful with the fruits. Cream the fat and sugar, add the honey and the eggs, one at a time, then the lemon juice and grated rind, fold in the flour and then the fruit and lastly the rum or orange juice. Line an 8-inch cake tin with 2 layers of brown paper and one of greaseproof paper, greased. Put the cake mixture into the tin and smooth the top. Bake at 300°F (145°C/Gas Mark 1) for 4 hours.

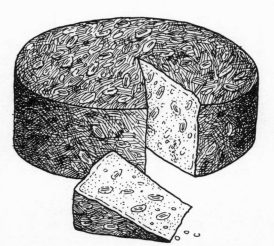

# DUTCH BISCUITS

½ lb (225g) self-raising 81 per cent flour
Pinch of salt
½ teaspoonful mixed spice
1 teaspoonful cinnamon
6 oz. (175g) margarine
5 oz. (150g) light brown sugar
Grated rind of ½ lemon
4 oz. (100g) ground almonds
1 oz. (25g) shortbread biscuit crumbs
Flaked almonds

Sieve the flour, salt and spices. Cream the fat and sugar and add the lemon rind and ground almonds, biscuit crumbs and flour. Mix and then knead until smooth. Roll out very thinly, less than ¼ inch thickness, and then cut into the shapes of your choice or into 2½-inch rounds. Scatter the flaked almonds on top and press them lightly into the biscuits. Bake on shallow oven trays at 350°F (175°C/Gas Mark 4) for 10-14 minutes. Lift off with a spatula and cool on a wire tray.

# GINGER BISCUITS

1¼ oz. (35g) ground ginger
12 oz. (350g) plain flour
6 oz. (175g) sifted light brown sugar
9 oz. (250g) margarine

Sieve the flour and ginger, stir in the sugar and then rub in the butter and knead until smooth. Roll out very thin and cut into rounds. Arrange on baking tins and bake at 375°F (190°C/Gask Mark 5) for 25-30 minutes.

# GINGERBREAD FEATHER CAKE

5 oz. (150g) light brown sugar
6 oz. (175g) margarine
$\frac{1}{2}$ lb (225g) dark treacle
2 eggs
9 oz. (250g) self-raising flour
$\frac{1}{2}$ teaspoonful bicarbonate of soda
$\frac{3}{4}$ teaspoonful ground ginger
1 teaspoonful cinnamon
$\frac{1}{2}$ teaspoonful nutmeg
6 tablespoonful stout or milk
6 tablespoonful water

Melt the fat with the sugar and treacle. Sift all the dry ingredients and then beat into the first mixture. Make the stout very hot and pour it in and mix. Pour everything into prepared tin. Bake at 350°F (175°C/Gas Mark 4) for 40-45 minutes. Do not turn out of the tin until cold, then put on a wire rack. It may be iced with butter icing or dusted with sieved light brown sugar. You need a tin $11\frac{1}{2}$ x 9 inches and it should be lined with greaseproof paper brushed with melted fat or oil. A dripping or roasting tin is right.

# HONEY CAKES

1 lb (450g) honey
1 lb (450g) plain 81 per cent flour
$\frac{1}{4}$ lb (100g) margarine
4 tablespoonful milk
1 teaspoonful bicarbonate of soda
2 teaspoonful crushed coriander seeds

Put the honey and margarine in a saucepan and heat until it bubbles, then pour into a bowl. Sift the flour and soda into this mixture, add the milk and then the crushed coriander seed. Wrap and chill. Roll out on a floured surface when well-chilled and form into cakes and bake on greased floured baking tins with shallow sides. Bake at 400°F (200°C/Gas Mark 6) for 15 minutes. Leave on the tins until cold, store in closed tins.

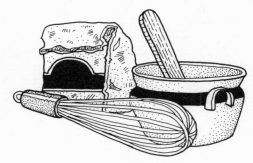

# HERB SCONES

4 oz. (100g) self-raising 81 per cent flour
2 oz. (50g) cooking fat
2 tablespoonful chosen herbs
Pinch of salt
Milk to mix

Rub the fat into the flour, add the herb and enough milk to make a soft dough then roll out to $\frac{3}{4}$-inch thickness and cut out as usual. Bake at 425°F (215°C/Gas Mark 8) for 10-12 minutes. Serve hot and buttered. These scones are very good placed on top of vegetable stews instead of dumplings.

## HERB BREAD

1 loaf of French bread
1 tablespoonful fresh herbs such as parsley,
    chives, marjoram, thyme, or chervil
2½ oz. (65g) margarine

Soften the margarine and mix in the minced herbs. Cut the loaf diagonally in ½-inch slices, but do not cut right through to the bottom crust. Spread each slice with some of the herb margarine. Press the loaf into shape again and wrap it in foil. Put in the oven at 425°F (215°C/Gas Mark 7) and bake for 15 minutes.

## POPPY SEED CAKE

1½ cupsful poppy seed
6 eggs, separated
1 cupful sugar
½ cupful mixed cut peel
1 teaspoonful allspice
Whipped cream
Pinch of salt

Grind the poppy seed in a blender, if you cannot buy it already ground. Beat the egg yolks until thick and pale and then, still beating, dribble in the sugar, stir in the spice, seed, salt and peel. Grease a spring form tin and pour the mixture into it. Heat the oven to 325°F (160°C/Gas Mark 3), put the cake into it and bake for 50 minutes. Leave the cake in the tin until cool, then remove the spring form. Spread the cake with whipped cream and serve at once.

## POUND CAKE

4 eggs
10 oz. (275g) 81 per cent flour
Grated rind of 1 lemon
8 oz. (225g) light brown sugar
8 oz. (225g) margarine
2 oz. (50g) cut peel
4 oz. (100g) currants
4 oz. (100g) sultanas

Cream the fat and sugar. Beat the eggs and add alternately with the flour to the creamed mixture. Mix well and then add the rest of the ingredients. Put in a greased floured tin and bake at 300°F (145°C/Gas Mark 2) for 2 hours.

## RICE CAKE

3 small eggs
2 oz. (50g) ground rice
4 oz. (100g) light brown sugar
1 teaspoonful baking powder
Good pinch of salt
4 oz. (100g) 81 per cent flour
4 oz. (100g) margarine
Grated rind of ½ lemon

Cream the fat and sugar, beat the eggs and add alternately with the flour and salt. Beat well then add the rice, lemon rind and baking powder. Line a tin with greaseproof paper and put the cake batter into it. Bake at 350°F (175°C/Gas Mark 4) for 25-30 minutes.

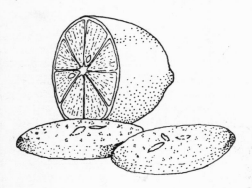

## NORWEGIAN COOKIES

Yolks of 3 hard-boiled eggs
4 oz. (100g) icing sugar
4 drops of almond essence
Good pinch of salt
6 tablespoonsful soft margarine
4 oz. (100g) flour
Blackberry jelly

Cream the fat and sugar and add the essence. Put the egg yolks through the blender or a sieve and add them. Mix the salt with the flour, add and mix well. Chill, wrapped in a plastic bag or cooking foil.

After about 1 hour, roll out very thinly and cut half with a 2½-inch round cutter then cut the rest of the biscuit dough with a cutter smaller than the first one. You will have a number of circles and rings with a hole in the centre; put the smaller rings on top of the larger. Bake at 350°F (175°C/Gas Mark 4) for 20 minutes and when cook spread with blackberry jelly. If you do not want to use the hard-boiled egg whites for any purpose, separate the eggs and drop the yolks into simmering water and cook for 10 minutes, after which time they should be firm.

## SEED SPONGE CAKE

3 eggs, separated
5 oz. (150g) light brown sugar
4 oz. (100g) self raising 81 per cent flour
1 dessertspoonful soft margarine
1½ tablespoonsful cornflour
1 tablespoonful orange flower water
2 tablespoonsful water
1 tablespoonful caraway seed
Pinch of salt

Beat the egg whites until stiff and dry and beat in the sugar to make a meringue texture. Mix the yolks in very gently. Sift the flour, salt and cornflour several times and fold lightly into the egg mixture. Heat the water, margarine and orange flower water, fold into the first mixture and add the caraway seeds. Grease and flour a cake tin and pour the cake batter into it; sprinkle with finely sieved sugar and bake at 400°F (200°C/Gas Mark 6) for 20 minutes.

## SPICED TEA CAKE

1 tablespoonful nutter
4 oz. (100g) sugar
4 oz. (100g) 81 per cent self-raising flour
½ pt. (275ml) milk
1 apple peeled, cored and sliced thinly
1 dessertspoonful crushed coriander seed
A little extra sugar
Nutmeg (optional)

Cream the fat and sugar, add the egg and beat well. Sift the flour with a pinch of salt and add it alternately with the milk. Grease and flour a cake tin and arrange the sliced apple on it; sprinkle with sugar, nutmeg and coriander seed. Pour the cake batter on top and bake at 350°F (175°C/Gas Mark 4) for about 30 minutes. Lift carefully out of the tin and put on a plate or a wire tray. May be eaten hot or cold.

## SAFFRON BUNS

Another very ancient recipe for a cake is Saffron Cake. Saffron is now terribly expensive as it takes 200,000 of the tiny stigmas of the special crocus to make one pound of saffron. This herb gave Saffron Walden its name and it features in the arms of that town. It was also grown in what is now a London street, Saffron Hill, which was once part of the gardens of Ely Place.

This herb now comes from different parts of the world and is almost as precious as gold dust. When you want to use saffron threads, crush the required number and soak them in the hot milk or liquid required by the recipe. When using the powdered saffron, it may be done the same way or sifted with flour. The following recipe is from Florence White's collection.

3½ lb (2kg) flour
½ lb (225g) margarine
½ pt. (275ml) top milk
2 large pinches saffron powder
3 eggs and 1 extra yolk
1 oz. (25g) dried yeast
8 oz. (225g) sugar
Salt
1 teaspoonful crushed coriander seeds

Warm the milk, margarine and sugar and then add the saffron. Mix the whole eggs and extra yolk with salt and yeast and coriander seeds. Let the milk mixture cool to lukewarm. Put the flour in a bowl and add the rest of the ingredients to it. Mix and then knead. Make into small cakes or buns let them rise until doubled in bulk, and then bake at 400°F (200°C/Gas Mark 6).

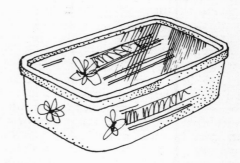

## SESAME AND OATMEAL COOKIES

4 oz. (100g) demerara sugar
4 oz. (100g) rolled oats
¼ cupful sesame seeds
1 level teaspoonful salt
¾ cupful desiccated coconut
4 oz. (100g) melted margarine

Mix all the dry ingredients together, add the melted butter and mix well. Press into a greased and floured tin (a swiss roll tin will do). Bake at 375°F (190°C/Gas Mark 5) for half an hour. Leave in the tin and cut into fingers when cold.

# SIMNEL CAKE

½ lb (225g) nutter or margarine
½ lb (225g) sieved sugar
3 large eggs
10 oz. (25g) self-raising 81 per cent flour
½ teaspoonful grated nutmeg
½ teaspoonful mixed spice
½ lb (225g) currants
3 oz. (75g) raisins
6 oz. (175g) sultanas
4 oz. (100g) cut mixed peel
2-3 oz. (50-75g) *glacé* cherries, halved
1 lb (450g) almond paste
Apricot jam

Cream the fat and sugar well then beat in the eggs one at a time. Sieve all the dry ingredients together, add to the creamed mixture then mix in the fruit. Grease and paper a round 8-inch cake tin and put half the cake mixture into it. Roll out part of the almond paste to a circle to fit the tin and put it on top of the cake mixture, then cover with the rest of the cake mixture. Bake at 350°F (175°C/Gas Mark 4) for 45 minutes then lower the heat to 320°F (160°C/Gas Mark 3) and bake for a further 2 hours. Do not turn out of the tin until the cake is cold. Then turn it upside down and spread with warmed apricot jam and put a neat round of almond paste on top. The rest of the paste, from the trimmings, should be rolled into twelve small balls (one for each of the Disciples) and fixed round the edge of the paste. Brown the top lightly under the grill.

# VELVET CHIFFON CAKE

5 eggs, separated
1½ cupsful sifted flour
1¾ teaspoonsful baking powder
1 level teaspoonful salt
1 cupful sugar
⅓ cupful salad oil
⅔ cupful juice from 2 oranges with water
2 tablespoonsful grated orange rind
¾ teaspoonful cream of tartar
Spare ¼ cupful of sugar

Sift together the flour, baking powder, salt and 1 cup of sugar; add salad oil, the liquid, grated orange peel and the un-beaten egg yolks and beat until smooth. Whisk the egg whites with the cream of tartar until they are stiff but not dry, then add half a cupful of sugar gradually. Beat to a very stiff meringue. Fold the egg yolk mixture delicately into the egg whites, making sure that it is perfectly blended. Turn into an ungreased tin and bake at 300°F (145°C/Gas Mark 2) for 65-70 minutes. Invert the tin when the cake is cooked but do not try to turn the cake out – it will drop out when it is ready.

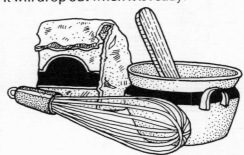

# WALNUT MACAROONS

4 egg whites
¼ teaspoonful salt
1 teaspoonful almond essence
¾ cupful sugar
3 cupsful crushed cornflakes
1 cupful coconut
1 cup coarsely-chopped walnuts

Add the salt to the egg whites and beat to a foam, not to a meringue texture. Add the sugar, a little at a time, and beat until you have a smooth, glossy mixture. Then fold in the cornflakes, coconut, almond essence and nuts, in that order. Drop from a teaspoon on to a well-greased tin. Bake at 350°F (175°C/Gas Mark 4) for about 15 minutes. Remove at once from the tin on to a wire tray.

# Chapter Six
# SALADS

A collection of salad dressings and mayonnaise is given at the end of this book: some of them can make plain lettuce a gastronomic treat. Unless directions are given to the contrary, the dressing is served separately.

## EGG BUTTERFLIES

4 large firm tomatoes
2 hard-boiled eggs
A little mustard and cress
Salad dressing

Wipe the tomatoes but do not skin. Place them stem sides down and then cut them in half almost to the bottom and then in half again, making 4 portions joined at the base. Spread apart gently and put a slice of egg between the tomato pieces. Put a little mustard and cress in the centre and serve on salad plates with more mustard and cress. Hand the dressing separately.

## STUFFED EGGS

3 hard-boiled eggs
Salad dressing
Pepper, salt and paprika
1 tomato
Lettuce and watercress

Shell the eggs carefully and cut them in halves lengthwise and remove the yolks carefully. If the eggs are turned several times while they are cooking then the yolks should be central and not all to one side as they are when left unturned.

Sieve or mash the yolks until they are free from lumps and mix with some of the chosen dressing to form a smooth piping consistency. Season with pepper and salt and put in a piping bag with a rose nozzle. Put a tiny piece of tomato in the centre of each egg slice or half then pipe the yolk mixture on it. Garnish with a little paprika and serve on a bed of lettuce or watercress.

## GOLDEN SALAD

Lettuce (of any kind)
1 lb (450g) cooked Jerusalem artichokes
3 hard-boiled eggs
Pinch of finely-chopped parsley
Pinch of chopped spring onion or chives
1 teaspoonful French mustard
1 tablespoonful white wine vinegar
2 tablespoonsful olive oil
Salt and pepper

Line a dish with lettuce leaves. Slice the cold artichokes thinly and arrange in the dish with the chopped egg whites, parsley and chives and sprinkle with a little extra vinegar to keep the artichokes white. Mash the egg yolks and slowly work in the mustard, vinegar and oil and pour over the vegetables. Serves four.

## ORATAVA SALAD

3 hard-boiled eggs
6 oz. (175g) cheddar cheese
2 eating apples
Little lemon juice
2 firm but ripe tomatoes
4 ripe bananas

Shell and slice the eggs and grate the cheese finely. Peel and core the apples and sprinkle with a little lemon juice. Peel and slice the tomatoes. Put the apple slices on a salad dish and cover with the sliced bananas. Then put alternate slices of tomato and egg round them and sprinkle with the cheese and pile the rest of the cheese in the middle. Serve with mayonnaise.

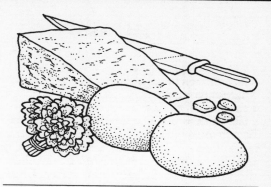

## EGG AND OLIVE SALAD

1 lettuce
2 hard-boiled eggs
2 tablespoonsful chopped ripe olives
2 tablespoonsful diced green pepper
1 tablespoonful finely-chopped chives
$\frac{1}{4}$ pt. (150ml) salad oil
2 tablespoonsful white wine vinegar or lemon juice
3 teaspoonsful sugar
1 teaspoonful each dry mustard, salt and paprika
Garlic to taste, finely minced

Shred the lettuce into a salad bowl. Press the eggs through a sieve and mix with the olives, green pepper and chives then put into the bowl with the lettuce. Make a dressing by mixing the oil, lemon juice or vinegar, sugar, salt, pepper and paprika and shake well. Pour over the salad and serve without delay.

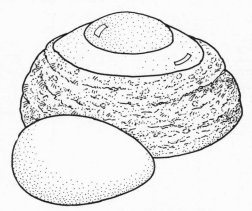

## ROSY SALAD

2 tablespoonsful brown sugar
$\frac{1}{4}$ pt. (150ml) lemon juice
4 cloves
$\frac{1}{2}$ teaspoonful salt
5-6 small cooked beetroots
6 hard-boiled eggs

Mix the lemon juice, cloves and salt. Peel and slice the beetroot, pour the first mixture over it and mix. Cook over very low heat for about 10 minutes. Leave to stand until nearly cold; add the sliced eggs and chill to serve very cold.

## SPANISH SALAD

1 large peeled garlic clove or 2 small ones
3 slices french bread, toasted
3 hard-boiled eggs
1 cos lettuce
3 tablespoonsful ripe olives, minced
French dressing

Rub the garlic on the toasted bread slices then cut the toast into small cubes. Chop the eggs finely. Tear the lettuce into bite-sized pieces. Mix the ingredients together and sprinkle with the dressing.

## EGG PEAR AND SULTANA SALAD

2 hard-boiled eggs
1 x 16 oz. (450g) tin of pears
2 lettuces with firm hearts
3 oz. (75g) finely-chopped celery
2 oz. (50g) chopped walnuts
3 oz. (75g) sultanas
1 level teaspoonful, salt, dash pepper
1 level teaspoonful sugar
2 tablespoonsful white wine vinegar
4 tablespoonsful salad oil
1 clove of garlic

Drain all the syrup from the pears and put the fruit into a bowl. Pour the vinegar over the pears and leave to stand while the rest of the salad is made. Cut the garlic clove and rub the inside of the bowl with the cut sides. Wash the lettuce and shred the leaves into the bowl. Then add the celery, walnuts, sultanas and sliced eggs. Lift the pears carefully out of the vinegar and put on top of the mixture in the bowl. Keep the drained-off liquid. Just before the salad is to be served, dress it with the mixed oil and vinegar with the sugar, salt and pepper added. Shake well. Serves 9-10 people.

## EGG AND CUCUMBER SALAD WITH SOUR CREAM

Whites of 3 hard-boiled eggs, chopped
1 cucumber
3 tablespoonsful chopped spring onions
Watercress
¾ teaspoonful made mustard
½ teaspoonful light brown sugar
2 dessertspoonsful fresh lemon juice
Salt and pepper
2 tablespoonsful olive oil
½ pt. (275ml) soured cream
Garnish with sieved yolks of the hard-boiled
  eggs

Slice the cucumber and mix with the onions, salad greens and chopped egg whites, using as much watercress or torn lettuce as you like. Cover and chill until needed. When serving, put the salad into a salad bowl, add a dressing made from the sour cream mixed with the mustard, sugar and lemon juice, add salt and pepper to taste and then blend in the oil. This may best be done in an electric blender. Put in a chilled bowl, sprinkle the sieved egg yolks on top and serve at once.

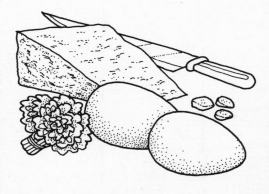

## DEVILLED EGG SALAD

6 large eggs
2 tablespoonsful thick cream or ideal milk or
  mayonnaise
1 teaspoonful french mustard
Dash of Worcester sauce
1 oz. (25g) butter
Salt

Boil the eggs for 10 minutes then shell them carefully and slice them lengthwise. Remove the yolks and mash them well. Cream the butter until it is very soft, then add the egg yolks, cream and mustard, Worcester sauce, salt and pepper to taste. Beat until smooth or blend it in a blender. It has to be of piping consistency. Pipe large rosettes into the egg whites and garnish with parsley and capers or sliced stuffed olives. Put a heap of watercress or endive in the centre of a round dish and surround with the filled eggs. A little red pepper or tomato may be added to give more colour.

## MOULDED CHEESE SALAD

½ breakfast cupful breadcrumbs, wholemeal or
  brown
½ oz. (15g) custard powder
½ pt. (275ml) milk
½ teaspoonful prepared mustard
Salt and pepper
3 oz. (75g) grated sharp cheese

Mix the crumbs with the custard powder and put into a pan; add the milk slowly and, when blended, add the mustard, salt and pepper and lastly the grated cheese and stir over very low heat until the mixture is well blended. Then raise the heat slightly and cook and stir until it boils. Then raise the heat slightly and cook and stir until it boils. Dampen small moulds and pour the mixture into them. Allow to cool and then put in the refrigerator until firm. Turn out on to lettuce leaves or use endive and watercress, or all three. Serve mayonnaise separately.

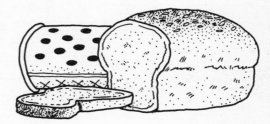

## CHEESE AND PRUNE SALAD

4 oz. (100g) cream cheese
2 teaspoonsful finely chopped chives
1 teaspoonful chopped parsley
1 teaspoonful chopped pickled gherkins
1 tablespoonful mayonnaise
12 large juice prunes
Lettuce
French dressing

Mix the first five ingredients together. Soak the prunes overnight in cold tea if possible, if not, in cold water. Remove the stones and fill the cavities with the cheese mixture. Toss the lettuce in the french dressing and arrange it in a bowl with the prunes on top.

## CHEESE AND CELERY SALAD

4 oz. (100g) cream cheese
2 tablespoonsful chopped celery
2 tablespoonsful chopped dessert apple
1 teaspoonful minced parsley
Celery sticks

Mix the first four ingredients together and arrange on a dish of lettuce. Place several sticks of celery at each end of the dish.

## POTTER'S SALAD

6 oz. (175g) short pastry
2 pears
2 oz. (50g) cream cheese
4 oz. (100g) cooked young carrots
4 tomatoes
Lettuce and dressing

Make the pastry from one of the recipes given or use your own favourite pastry. Roll it out and line a flan ring or tin with it. Bake in the preheated oven at 425°F (215°C/Gas Mark 7) for about 15-20 minutes until golden brown. Be sure to prick the base of the pastry flan first or it will rise in a hump. Put aside to cool.

Peel and core the pears and halve them. Place them in the flan case, cut sides up and fill the hollows with cream cheese. Skin and slice the tomatoes and slice the carrots and put in the spaces between the pears. Put a few dabs of dressing or mayonnaise here and there. Serve with a bowl of lettuce or mixed salad greens.

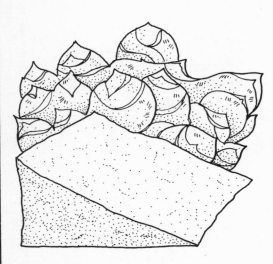

## CHEESE SALAD BOWL

5 oz. (150g) sliced cooked waxy potatoes
4 oz. (100g) shredded raw white cabbage
1 eating apple, cored and diced
2 tablespoonsful chopped mixed pickles
4 oz. (100g) cheddar cheese, cut in small cubes
Salad dressing to taste
Lettuce or any other salad greens

Mix the ingredients together and blend them with the dressing. Serve piled in a bowl on the chosen saladings.

## SOUR CREAM AND POTATO SALAD

1½ lb (675g) diced, cooked potatoes
3 oz. (75g) diced cucumber (with the skin on)
1 dessertspoonful minced mild onion
½ teaspoonful celery seed
1½ teaspoonful sea salt
3 hard-boiled eggs
Generous ½ pt. (275ml) soured cream
4 tablespoonful salad cream or mayonnaise
⅛ pt. (75ml) vinegar
1 level teaspoonful made mustard
Grated cheese
Lettuce or other saladings

Mix the first six ingredients together and toss gently. Separate the egg yolks from the whites, dice the whites and add to the first ingredients. Mash the egg yolks and mix with the sour cream, mustard, vinegar and mayonnaise then mix lightly into the potato mixture. Leave to stand in a cold place for 15 minutes to allow the flavours to blend. Serve dusted with grated cheese on lettuce or other greens.

## CHEESE AND CARROT SALAD

1 medium carrot
2 tablespoonful grated cheese
1 tablespoonful french dressing

Shred the carrot and mix it with the dressing and either mix in the cheese or scatter it on top. Serve on lettuce. Enough for one serving.

## SWISS CHESSE AND POTATO SALAD

1 lb (450g) Swiss cheese
5 medium-sized potatoes, cooked
3 oz. (75g) minced onion
½ teaspoonful salt, dash pepper
Scant ½ pt. (275ml) french dressing

Cut the cheese and potatoes into small cubes and then mix with the rest of the ingredients. Chill for one hour. Serve on or with any green salad. Serves eight.

## CREAM CHEESE AND PEANUT SALAD

1-2 large lettuces
6 oz. (175g) cream cheese
4 tablespoonful french dressing
3 oz. (75g) finely chopped peanuts

Reserve 4 large leaves of the lettuce and tear up the rest. Mix the cheese, french dressing and half the peanuts. Mix with the shredded lettuce. Line a salad bowl with the large lettuce leaves, put the mixture in the middle and sprinkle the rest of the nuts on top. Serves six.

## MACARONI CHEESE SALAD

6 oz. (175g) uncooked macaroni
1 cut clove of garlic
1 bottle of olives, stoned and chopped
6 oz. (175g) diced celery
4 oz. (100g) diced green pepper
6 tomatoes, cut in wedges
6 oz. (175g) diced cheddar cheese
French dressing

Cook the macaroni in boiling salted water until just tender (about 15-20 minutes). Rub a salad bowl with the garlic. Mix the next five ingredients together, put into the salad bowl and coat with the dressing so that it glistens. Cover and chill for not less than one hour. Serve on or with lettuce or other salad greens. Serves from six to eight.

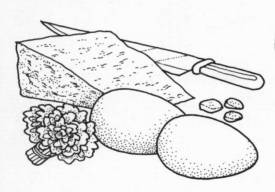

## TOMATO ROSE SALAD

8 firm, fair-sized tomatoes
$\frac{3}{4}$ lb (325g) cream cheese
Milk
2 hard-boiled egg yolks
Watercress
Lettuce leaf cups
French dressing

Peel the tomatoes and chill them. Soften the cheese with milk (only practice will tell you how soft it must be). Form a row of two petals on each tomato by pressing small teaspoons filled level with the cream cheese and milk texture. Do not make the mixture too soft or the petals will not stay put. Press the teaspoon against the side of the tomato then draw it down with a curving motion. It is a good idea to try this out on a potato or some other round object until you can make the petals with ease. Cover the tomato with the petals. Sprinkle the centre of each 'rose' with sieved egg yolk. Put each 'rose' on a lettuce leaf formed into a cup shape and garnish with a few watercress leaves. Do not be discouraged if you do not make a perfect rose the first time: the knack will come. Serves eight.

## AVOCADO SURPRISE

2 large avocados
6 tablespoonsful cottage cheese
2 tablespoonsful chopped walnuts
2 tablespoonsful minced olives
2 tablespoonsful minced chives
Lettuce
French dressing

Cut the avocados in halves lengthwise and remove the stones. Remove the skins very carefully. Mix the cheese, olives, chives and nuts and fill the cavities in the avocados with the mixture. Then place the halves together again, wrap in waxed paper and put into the refrigerator for three hours. To serve: cut into very thin slices and serve on lettuce leaves then sprinkle with the dressing. Serves four.

## WINTER SALAD

½ lb (225g) cheddar cheese, grated
24 marshmallows, cut in quarters (optional)
4 tablespoonsful green maraschino cherries,
   chopped
1 small tin crushed pineapple, drained
Scant ½ pt. (275ml) mayonnaise
Scant ½ pt. (275ml) double cream, whipped
6-8 green pepper rings
Watercress

Mix together all the ingredients except the green pepper rings and watercress. Toss lightly together to blend well. This mixture may now either be pressed into small individual moulds or spread in a shallow tin. Chill overnight until firm. Cut into squares or turn out of the moulds and serve on individual plates of watercress and top each serving with a green pepper ring. Cottage cheese may be used instead of cheddar; it is so much milker, and, I think, nicer. Broken walnuts may be substituted for the marshmallows. Serves six to eight.

## VEGETABLE MAYONNAISE

¼ light-cooked medium cauliflower or a small
   whole one
4 cooked waxy potatoes
2 cooked carrots
4 gherkins
1 hard-boiled egg
6 oz. (175g) cooked green peas
1 small tin butter beans
Salad cream or mayonnaise
Watercress
2 cooked beets
Celery
Lettuce

Cook the cauliflower *very* lightly and divide it into florets. Dice the potatoes and carrots, chop the gherkins and egg and mix all together with the peas and beans and bind with mayonnaise. Line a bowl with lettuce leaves, pile the vegetables in it and garnish with watercress. Surround the salad with slices of beetroot and celery curls.

## AVOCADO CHEESE SALAD

2 British Standard measuring cupsful diced
   avocado
1 cupful sliced celery
½ cupful crumbled blue cheese
1 cupful mayonnaise
2 teaspoonsful lemon juice
Lettuce

Mix the ingredients, except the lettuce, in the order given and serve on lettuce.

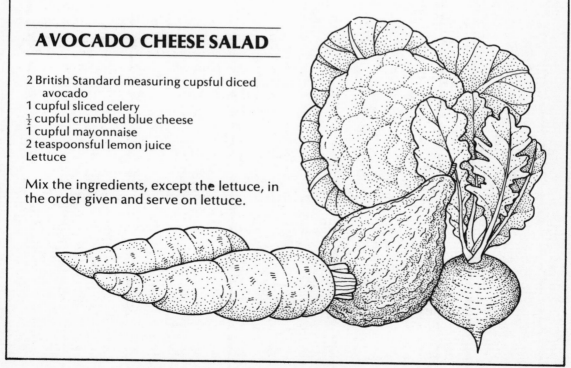

## STUFFED TOMATO SALAD

4-5 large tomatoes
1 grated onion
3 oz. (75g) raw rice
Salad dressing
Salt and pepper
5 lightly-cooked mushrooms
Some stuffed olives

Cut the tops off the tomatoes and scoop out the pulp. Then chop the pulp and mix with the onion. Have the rice cooked and very cold, mix it in and bind with the salad dressing; season to taste. Chop up a few of the olives and keep some for garnish. Fill the tomatoes with this mixture. Line a dish with lettuce leaves and put the tomatoes on it in a ring and arrange the mushrooms in between the tomatoes, caps up. Garnish the tomatoes with some sliced olives and watercress.

## SLICED POTATO SALAD

6 medium-sized waxy potatoes, cooked
   carefully, sliced
2 spring onions, minced
Mayonnaise
Finely-chopped parsley
Mustard and cress

Mix the potatoes and onions and blend in some mayonnaise. Pile on a dish lined with lettuce, sprinkle generously with parsley and garnish with mustard and cress.

## BROCCOLI SALAD

8 oz. (225g) broccoli
1 small onion, chopped
1 teaspoonful minced capers
2 tomatoes
Salad cream

Break the broccoli into sprigs or stalks and cook lightly in boiling salted water then rinse in cold water. Put into a bowl, cover and stand it in the refrigerator for 20 minutes. Prepare the onion and capers and mix them with some salad cream and then pour over the chilled broccoli. Cut the tomatoes into wedges and garnish with them.

## NEW CARROT AND ONION SALAD

¾ lb (325g) new little carrots
2 small onions or 6 spring onions
Parsley
Mayonnaise
Mustard and cress

Cook the carrots in boiling salted water –
do them very lightly so that they are crisp.
When they are cold cut them into slices.
Cut the onions into thin rings and mix
with the carrots. Chop some parsley, just
as much or as little as you like, and mix it
with the mayonnaise and then bind the
vegetables with it. Serve on mustard and
cress.

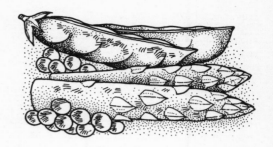

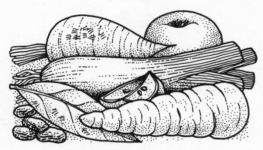

## STUFFED ARTICHOKE SALAD

4 globe artichokes
4 tomatoes of even size
Salt and pepper
Mayonnaise
2 hard-boiled eggs
Watercress

Choose small young tender artichokes,
cut off the stalks and trim the leaves. Have
a pan ready with a little boiling water in it
and a little vinegar or lemon juice. Cook
the artichokes gently until just tender,
drain and leave to cool. Remove the inner
leaves and centres. Skin and chop the
tomatoes and season them; then fill the
cavities in the artichokes with them.
Garnish to taste with eggs and watercress.

## COLESLAW (1)

½ small firm white cabbage
3 stalks celery
Salad cream

Wash the cabbage and cut into into
quarters, then slice *very* thinly. Put the
cabbage slices into ice cold water and
then into the refrigerator for 15 minutes,
then drain and dry carefully. Chop the
celery very finely and mix with the
cabbage, adding salad cream to blend
them together. If preferred, the following
ingredients may be added: chopped
apple, chopped nuts, blanched raisins or
sultanas.

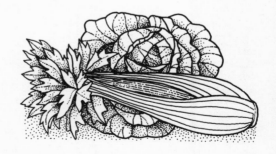

## COLESLAW (2)

1 small head white cabbage
½ pt. (275ml) mayonnaise
1 or more teaspoonsful french mustard
1 teaspoonful castor sugar
A little sliced onion or green pepper

Use only the heart of the cabbage and shred it finely after washing it carefully. Then put it into cold water until it is crisp. Drain and dry it and chill in a bowl in the refrigerator. Mix the mustard with the mayonnaise, add the sugar then blend into the chilled cabbage. Pile on a serving dish and garnish with chopped onion or green pepper.

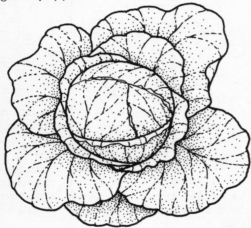

Prepare the cabbage after washing it, drain and put in the refrigerator to crisp. Do not assemble this salad until just before serving time, then toss in the chosen fruit, dribble the honey over it and add the rest of the ingredients. About half a measuring cupful of sour cream will be needed. If you like the flavour, powdered anise gives a delightful and unusual flavour to this salad.

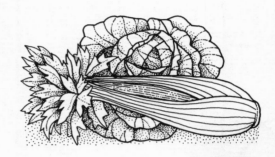

## COLESLAW WITH FRUIT

2-3 British Standard measuring cupsful of
   grated raw white cabbage
2 tablespoonsful honey
4 tablespoonsful soured cream
¼ cupful minced green pepper
Salt and pepper
Lemon juice
Powdered fennel (optional)
*Choose from:*
Seedless grapes, or
Cantaloup or melon balls, or
Sliced fresh peaches, or
Sour apple sticks, or
Stoned cherries

## STUFFED CABBAGE SALAD

1 medium white cabbage
1 medium red cabbage of equal size
Mayonnaise or salad cream
1 clove of garlic
Grated cheddar cheese

Trim the outside leaves off the cabbage. Wash and dry the cabbage hearts and level off the bases so that they will stand on them. Cut a round from the top of each cabbage and scoop out the centre of each one with a sharp pointed knife. Shred the centres separately. Mix each portion generously with mayonnaise, with which the finely minced garlic has been mixed. Then fill the cavity in the red cabbage with the white cabbage and vice versa. Serve side by side on a generous bed of grated cheese.

# TOMATO AND AVOCADO SALAD

4 tablespoonsful olive or salad oil
4 tablespoonsful lemon juice
4 tomatoes, skinned and cut into eighths
2 large avocados
¼ teaspoonful salt
1 clove garlic, cut in half
1 crisp lettuce
6 stalks of chicory
1 head of endive

Pour the oil and 2 tablespoonsful of the lemon juice over the tomatoes and then put into the refrigerator. Cut the avocados into halves lengthwise and remove the stones. Peel, and then cut the fruit into crescents and sprinkle them with the rest of the oil and lemon and a sprinkle of salt. Rub a salad bowl with the cut garlic and shred the salad greens into the bowl, add the tomatoes and mix carefully. Sprinkle the dressing over the top. Serves six to eight.

# AUTUMN SALAD

1 small firm white cabbage
1 finely chopped mild onion
2 oz. (50g) sultanas
2 raw carrots, grated
4 oz. (100g) diced cheddar cheese

Remove the outside leaves from the cabbage and wash it and then drain well. Shred the cabbage finely and then mix all the ingredients together. Serves four.

# BROAD BEAN SALAD

1 lettuce
1 lb (450g) cooked, cold broad beans
4 inches of cucumber
3 tomatoes
½ lb (225g) cooked green peas
3 artichoke hearts
Few young spinach leaves, raw
French dressing

Arrange the lettuce leaves on a round flat dish. Put the broad beans in the centre. Slice the artichoke hearts, arrange them round the beans then arrange the rest of the vegetables in a tasteful fashion. Just before serving, sprinkle with the dressing. Serves four.

# FRESH BEET SALAD

2-3 small uncooked beets
A little olive oil
Fresh lemon juice
1 lettuce
Chopped parsley

Scrub the raw beet and take off the skin, then mix in a little oil and fresh lemon juice. Pile on lettuce leaves and garnish with parsley. Have the beet shredded very finely.

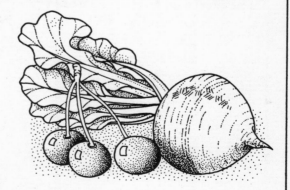

## MUSHROOM SALAD

8 oz. (225g) boiled, cold, sliced potatoes
6 oz. (175g) raw button mushrooms
Watercress
4 sticks celery, sliced
4 hard-boiled eggs, sliced
Mayonnaise

Reserve two of the eggs and then mix all the ingredients together. Do this carefully so that the egg slices are not mashed up. Add mayonnaise and mix gently again. Garnish with the other 2 eggs, sliced or cut in wedges.

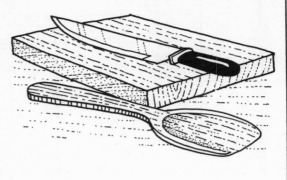

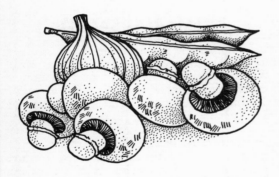

## BEAN SPROUTS AND WATERCRESS SALAD

Wash and drain the bean sprouts (fresh or tinned). To each measuring cupful of sprouts add $\frac{1}{4}$ cupful of sliced water chestnuts, $\frac{1}{2}$ cupful pineapple chunks and $\frac{1}{4}$ cupful slivered green pepper. Make a dressing from 1 cupful mayonnaise mixed with 1 teaspoonful each of soy sauce and curry powder. Mix well and then mix carefully with the first ingredients. Arrange lettuce in a bowl and divide the salad between them. Sprinkle with toasted almonds. Serves six.

## SPINACH SALAD WITH NUT DRESSING

$\frac{3}{4}$ British Standard measuring cupful nuts (pine nuts or cashew or walnuts)
3 tablespoonsful olive oil
3 tablespoonsful tarragon vinegar
$\frac{1}{4}$ teaspoonful grated lemon rind
$\frac{1}{4}$ teaspoonful salt
Dash of nutmeg
$2\frac{1}{2}$ pt. ($1\frac{1}{2}$l) freshly torn young spinach leaves, raw

Mix the first 6 ingredients and then mix lightly with the spinach leaves. Serves six.

## ORIENTAL SALAD

¼ pt. (150ml) salad soil
3 tablespoonsful tarragon vinegar
3 tablespoonsful tomato ketchup
2 tablespoonsful castor sugar
1 tablespoonful lemon juice
¼ teaspoonful salt
½ teaspoonful paprika
¼ teaspoonful garlic salt
½ lb (225g) fresh young spinach leaves
6 oz. (175g) tin bamboo shoots
6 oz. (175g) tinned water chestnuts

Stir the oil slowly into the vinegar, add the ketchup, sugar, lemon juice, salt, pepper, paprika and garlic salt, stir vigorously then chill. Tear the spinach leaves into small pieces and put in a salad bowl. Slice the water chestnuts and bamboo shoots thinly and put alternately with the bean sprouts on the bed of spinach. Shake the dressing and pour over the salad. Sieve the egg on top and sprinkle with sesame seeds. Serves six.

## CELERIAC SALAD BOWL

3 lb (1¼kg) celeriac (about 4 roots)
3 oz. (75g) diced celery
2 oz. (50g) chopped walnuts
2 tablespoonsful seedless raisins
2 tablespoonsful minced chives
2 tablespoonsful chopped green pepper
2 tablespoonsful stuffed green olives cut in halves
6 tablespoonsful mayonnaise
1 level teaspoonful salt
¼ teaspoonful Tabasco
2 tablespoonsful tarragon vinegar
Dash of pepper
Endive or cos lettuce or Webb's Wonderful
½ pt. (275ml) soured cream
Paprika (if liked)

Scrub the celeriac roots, put them in a pan and cover with boiling water. Put a lid on the pan and simmer for about half an hour until they are just tender, not soft. Drain, cool, peel and dice. Now mix with the next 6 ingredients, sprinkle with salt and blend with mayonnaise mixed with the Tabasco, vinegar and pepper. Then chill the mixture. Line a dish or bowl with the salad greens chosen and mound the salad on it. Swirl thick soured cream on top and dust with paprika. Serves from six to eight.

## YOGURT AND CUCUMBER SALAD

1 large cucumber
½ pt. (275ml) yogurt
4 teaspoonsful freshly-chopped mint
Salt to taste

Peel the cucumber and slice very thinly (a potato peeler is good for this job). Blend the yogurt, mint and salt, adding a touch of garlic if liked. Mix with the cucumber and chill for at least one hour before serving it. Serves from four to five.

## CUCUMBER AND APRICOT SALAD

2 ridge cucumbers
1 teaspoonful salt
1 teaspoonful castor sugar or light brown sugar
4 tablespoonsful syrup from tinned apricots
2 tablespoonsful tarragon vinegar
½ teaspoonful fresh tarragon or 1 teaspoonful
    dried tarragon
Dash of pepper
Any salad greens
Some slices of cucumber for garnish

Peel the cucumbers and slice them paper-thin into a salad bowl. Sprinkle the salt over them, put a plate or saucer on the cucumbers and a weight on top of it and leave to stand at room temperature for 6-8 hours. Drain off the water as it collects. Mix the apricot syrup, tarragon, vinegar, sugar and pepper and taste, add more vinegar if the dressing is too sweet.

About one hour before the salad is to be served pour the dressing over the cucumbers and mix lightly. Cover, and put the salad into the refrigerator for one hour. Then turn it into a chilled bowl lined with crisp lettuce leaves, also well chilled. Garnish with spare cucumber slices.

## GREEN PEA SALAD

1½ British Standard measuring cupsful cooked
    green peas
5 oz. (150g) diced celery
3 hard-boiled eggs, sliced or chopped
¼ pt. (150ml) mayonnaise
4 oz. (100g) chopped peanuts
3 tomatoes, skinned and sliced
Lettuce

Mix the peas, celery and egg and cover, then chill. Line 6 plates with lettuce leaves and divide the peas, etc., between them. Drop spoonsful of mayonnaise on each salad and garnish with sliced tomatoes and peanuts.

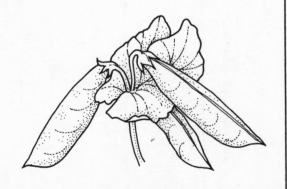

## WALNUT AND CABBAGE SALAD

1 small tight cabbage
1 avocado, diced
1 carrot, grated
5 oz. (150g) chopped walnuts
4 spring onions, sliced
Garlic salt (if liked)
¼ pt. (150ml) mayonnaise
½ tablespoonful made mustard
Juice of 1 lemon and a little of the grated rind

Shred the cabbage finely and mix with the next 5 ingredients. Blend in the mayonnaise, mustard and lemon juice mixed with the other ingredients. Serve in a bowl with the grated lemon rind on top. Serves six.

## TROPICAL SALAD

1 medium-sized firm cabbage
4 oz. (100g) flaked coconut
Carton of soured cream
2½ dessertspoonsful vinegar or lemon juice
½ teaspoonful salt
3 teaspoonsful sugar
Toasted coconut
Paprika

Shred the cabbage finely and mix with the coconut. Mix the soured cream, vinegar, salt and sugar then toss with the first ingredients. When well mixed, sprinkle with toasted coconut and paprika. To toast coconut: spread a thin layer on a baking tin and put in the oven set at 350°F (175°C/Gas Mark 4) and toast for 3-4 minutes. Watch carefully for it burns easily.

## BEETROOT AND CURRY POWDER SALAD

¼ pt. (150ml) vinegar or lemon juice
¼ pt. (150ml) salad oil
1 teaspoonful sugar
Salt
½ teaspoonful curry powder
1 tin diced beetroot, drained
5 oz. (150g) diced raw onion

Take a jar with a screw top and in it mix the vinegar, salad, oil, sugar, salt and curry powder; shake well until mixed. Mix the beetroot and onion and then blend in the dressing. Put into the refrigerator for several hours. Looks good served in lettuce cups.

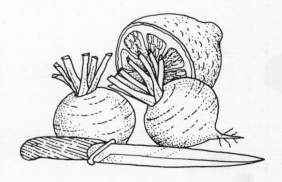

## GREEN PEPPER RING SALAD

Endive and crisp cos lettuce
2 large green peppers, de-seeded and cut in rings
2 medium-sized onions sliced and pressed into rings
¼ pt. (150ml) sour french dressing

Line 5-6 salad plates with the endive and shredded lettuce then arrange alternate rings of pepper and onion on them. Serves five or six.

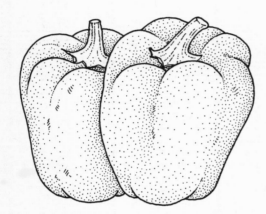

## MUSHROOM AND OLIVE SALAD

½ teaspoonful salt
1 dessertspoonful water
1 clove of garlic, minced
6 tablespoonsful salad oil
3 dessertspoonsful vinegar
2 teaspoonsful lemon juice
1 level teaspoonful sugar
¼ teaspoonful each of dry mustard, rosemary, (dried) and Worcester sauce
4 oz. tin (100g) or 4 oz. (100g) tiny button mushrooms, fresh
1 lettuce, torn into pieces
3 oz. (75g) diced celery
4 spring onions, chopped
1 heaped tablespoonful minced parsley
6 tablespoonsful stuffed olives, sliced

Dissolve the salt in the water, add the garlic and leave to stand for not less than half an hour; stir now and then. Mix the oil and vinegar, lemon juice, sugar, mustard, rosemary, Worcester sauce and then add the mushrooms. Strain the garlic and add the water to the dressing and mix it in, then leave to stand for 20 minutes for the flavours to blend. Lift out the mushrooms and arrange with the rest of the ingredients in a salad bowl, sprinkle on the dressing and mix lightly. Serves five or six.

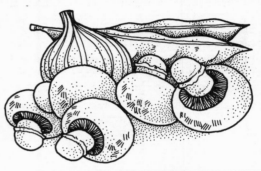

## BEAN SPROUT AND TOMATO SALAD

6 firm ripe tomatoes
1 lb 4 oz. (550g) bean sprouts
1 dessertspoonful parsley or chervil, minced
1 green pepper, de-seeded and chopped
3 stalks of celery, sliced thinly
Salt and pepper
Mayonnaise
Paprika
Lettuce

Scoop out the centres of the tomatoes and level the stem ends so that they will stand. Chop the pulp and season it with salt and leave to drain, upside down in the refrigerator. Drain off any surplus liquid from the chopped pulp and mix with the chopped bean sprouts and the rest of the ingredients. Moisten with mayonnaise and then stuff the icy cold tomatoes with this mixture and put a dash of paprika on the top of each one. Serve on a long dish lined with crisp lettuce leaves and hearts. Serves six.

## RUSSIAN SALAD

3 carrots sliced thinly
3 oz. (75g) runner beans or french beans, diced
2 waxy potatoes, cooked and diced
3 oz. (75g) cooked green peas
Mayonnaise
Lemon juice (about 1 teaspoonful)
Salt and pepper

If the carrots and beans are very young they may be used raw, but otherwise just cook them slightly. Mix the lemon juice into the mayonnaise. Mix the other ingredients together and then bind with mayonnaise. Serves two.

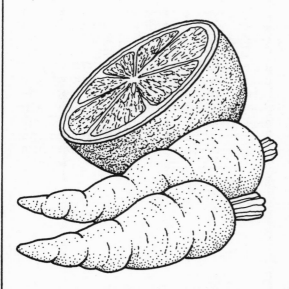

## RED CABBAGE SALAD

1 firm red cabbage
2 tablespoonsful chopped green pepper
3 tablespoonsful minced chives
2 tablespoonsful celery, sliced very thinly
2 tablespoonsful vegetarian sausage sliced in ½-inch slices

Shred the cabbage and mix with the rest of the ingredients. Blend with french dressing.

## DANDELION SALAD

4-6 oz. (100-175g) dandelion leaves, young ones only
2 hard-boiled egg yolks
1 level teaspoonful french mustard
Salt, pepper, paprika
1 tablespoonful garlic or tarragon vinegar
3 tablespoonsful olive or salad oil

Use only the young dandelion leaves picked when the flowers are just in bud in the spring. Trim them, wash and dry them. Pulverize the egg yolks and add the rest of the ingredients in the order given and mix well until blended. Do not add the dandelion leaves until just before serving.

## DANDELION AND ORANGE SALAD

Dandelion leaves (as above)
Orange peel
Sour cream
Made mustard
Vinegar
Salt and pepper
Lettuce

Tear up the dandelion or endive leaves. Cut some paper-thin slices of orange peel and then cut into the finest strips using sharp scissors. Boil the peel for 5 minutes which removes the bitterness. Chill. When cold, mix with the dandelion leaves or endive. Mix all the seasonings to taste with the sour cream and then pour over the other ingredients, mix and serve.

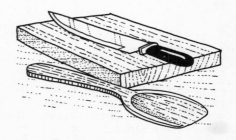

## SALSIFY AND TOMATO SALAD

Peel some ripe tomatoes, red or yellow ones and cut them into small pieces. Cook salsify in boiling salted water then cut into small pieces, dress with french dressing and chill well. Then mix with the tomatoes and serve on crisp lettuce.

## BEET ASPIC

8 young beets, the size of a golfball
¾ pt. (425ml) warm water
6 cloves
2 dessertspoonsful honey
Salt and pepper
Plain gelozone or aspic powder
Juice of 1 lemon, strained
Orange, lemon or grapefruit, strained
¼ pt. (150ml) white or red wine

Wash the beets carefully but do not skin them. Grate them into the warm water, add the cloves and simmer for 20 minutes. Strain the liquid off the beets but do not press it or it will be cloudy. Add the honey and seasonings. Soak the gelozone in the lemon juice, allowing 1 teaspoonful of gelozone for each ½ pt. (275ml) of liquid. If six cups are required, measure the beet juice and add enough fruit juice to make 5 cups – this will allow space for the wine.

Heat the beet juice and soak the steeped gelozone in it then allow it to melt. When it is cool add the wine. Divide between either small rinsed moulds or put all into a ring mould and chill until firm. Serve with lettuce and any preferred garnish.

## ITALIAN SALAD

5 oz. (150g) cooked carrots
3 oz. (75g) cooked young turnips, diced
5 oz. (150g) cooked potatoes, diced
5 oz. (150g) tomatoes, skinned and diced
3 oz. (75g) chopped french or runner beans
4 oz. (100g) cooked green peas
6 olives, stoned and chopped
12 capers
2 tablespoonsful finely chopped parsley
Mayonnaise
Hard-boiled eggs, sliced, for garnish

Mix all but the eggs and blend with mayonnaise, garnish with the eggs. In Italy they would add anchovy fillets but the salad tastes fine without them.

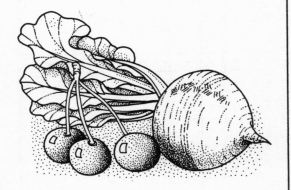

# CAULIFLOWER SALAD

1 young cauliflower, lightly cooked and chilled
4 hard-boiled eggs, cut in quarters
5 oz. (150g) cooked green peas
4 oz. (100g) cooked broad beans
2 level dessertspoonsful capers
1 courgette cooked in garlic and oil, chilled
    and sliced
Chicory
French dressing or mayonnaise

Separate the cauliflower into little sprigs. Mix the next 4 ingredients together, put them on a bed of chicory and then put the eggs on top. It is a good idea to mix the dressing and mayonnaise together; it makes a spicy dressing which may be spread on top of the eggs. This is an excellent salad for a party because it is so easy to make it to any size.

# IRON CURTAIN CHICORY SALAD

Salad bowl full of chicory or endive
6 tablespoonsful thick mayonnaise
4 tablespoonsful tomato sauce
3 or more tablespoonsful soured cream
1 tablespoonful creamed horseradish

Mix the ingredients lightly and then toss with the chicory or endive. I think endive would be my first choice.

# SALADE DE PANAIS

4 young parsnips (after the frost has touched
    them) cooked lightly
3 oz. (75g) cooked green peas
5 oz. (150g) sliced celery hearts
Mayonnaise
Lettuce

Peel the parsnips and chill them with the other vegetables. Then cut the parsnips into $\frac{1}{2}$-inch thick rounds and cut out the cores if they are at all hard. Then toss all together and moisten with mayonnaise. Serve on a generous bed of crisp lettuce.

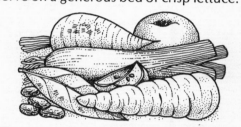

# RICE AND GREEN PEA SALAD

6 oz. (175g) brown or long grain rice
1 pt. (550ml) vegetable stock
1 level teaspoonful turmeric
$2\frac{1}{2}$ lb ($1\frac{1}{4}$kg) cooked green peas
1 lb (450g) spring onions
4 tablespoonsful olive oil
Garnish of chopped chives or parsley

Mix the turmeric with stock and bring to the boil; taste and season. Add the rice, cover the pan and cook at the lowest possible heat for 45 minutes, then remove the lid from the pan and leave it until the liquid has evaporated or soaked into the rice. Turn the rice into a large bowl and leave to cool. Cook the peas and prepare the spring onions. When all the ingredients are cold, mix together and coat with the oil. Cover and put in the refrigerator for 15 minutes and then serve. No more dressing is needed. Serves eight.

# COURGETTE SALAD

3 small courgettes
2 cloves of garlic, crushed
4 tablespoonsful olive oil
French dressing
Mixed salad greens
Garnish with minced spring onions and 4
    tablespoonsful Parmesan cheese

Wipe the courgettes, cut off the ends and slice into one inch pieces. Steam over boiling water for *2 minutes* then put the pieces on a plate or tin, but be careful not to let them overlap or they will become limp. Leave to cool and then put in the refrigerator for 15 minutes. Mix the oil and garlic. 15 minutes before mixing the salad, marinate the courgettes in the garlic oil for a few minutes. Then mix carefully with the salad greens adding more oil if needed. For the garnish, mix the onions and the grated cheese and sprinkle over the top.

# KOHLRABI AND CARROT SALAD

Part of a medium-sized kohlrabi
1 small onion
1 teaspoonful lemon juice
1 tablespoonful mayonnaise
½ teaspoonful brown sugar
1 teaspoonful chopped parsley
1 raw carrot

Peel the kohlrabi and carrot and then shred them on a coarse grater. Mix all the ingredients together. Another salad for one.

# LEEK, TOMATO AND APPLE SALAD

1 small leek (white part only)
1 small cooking apple
1 small yellow tomato
1 teaspoonful lemon juice
½ teaspoonful sugar
1 tablespoonful mayonnaise

Wash all grit out of the leek and cut it into thin slices, crosswise. Skin the apple and remove the core, then slice it. Cut the slices into small dice. Peel the tomato and dice it. Mix all the ingredients together. Serves one.

## CARROT AND RAISIN SALAD

2 oz. (50g) seedless raisins
5 oz. (150g) shredded raw carrot
2 oz. (50g) finely-sliced celery
2 oz. (50g) walnuts
Salt
2 dessertspoonsful mayonnaise

Soak the raisins in hot water for 15 minutes, then drain and cool them and mix with the other ingredients and chill well. Serve on lettuce or endive. Serves four.

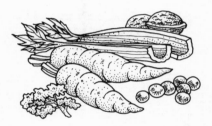

## GRAPEFRUIT AND LETTUCE CUP SALAD

1 grapefruit
2 heaped teaspoonsful sugar
1 teaspoonful french dressing
6 whole walnut halves
Lettuce

Prepare the grapefruit as follows: take a pair of kitchen scissors and a basin and with the scissors cut a vandyke or zigzag round the fruit in the middle then loosen the tips with the fingers, very gently, and carefully pull off half the skin, thus leaving the whole fruit in half the skin. Now remove the fruit in one piece from the half skin and put it in a basin. Remove all pith and skin from the whole fruit leaving the segments quite free. Sprinkle sugar on the fruit and replace it in the skin 'cup'. Chill well. Sprinkle with dressing; garnish with the walnuts and serve on lettuce. Serves one.

## ORANGE AND ONION SALAD

1 large Jaffa orange
1 grapefruit
French dressing
*Glacé* cherries
Watercress
1 mild onion, cut in paper-thin rings

Cut the orange and grapefruit into slices before they are skinned, then remove the peel and white pith with kitchen scissors. This is much easier than trying to cut neat slices when the skin has been removed. Sprinkle with the dressing and arrange in a very cold dish. Put a cherry in the centre of each slice and surround with the onion rings and water cress.

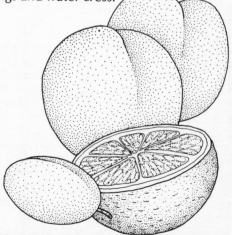

## CALIFORNIAN SALAD

4 inches of cucumber
3 tablespoonsful chopped celery
2 dessert apples, cored and sliced
2 bananas
4 tomatoes
Salt
Lemon juice
Mayonnaise or salad cream
Lettuce

Do not peel the cucumber: dice it with the celery. Slice the apple and sprinkle with lemon juice. Slice the skinned bananas and tomatoes thinly and sprinkle with salt, mix all together and mask with mayonnaise or salad cream and pile on a bed of shredded lettuce. Serves four.

## PEAR SALAD WITH GINGER CHEESE

6 pear halves, tinned or fresh
3 oz. (75g) cream cheese
2 tablespoonsful thick cream
3 tablespoonsful chopped crystallized ginger
Watercress or endive

Drain the pear halves and chill them; if fresh ones are used, skin and core them first. Soften the cream cheese with the cream and add the finely chopped ginger. Heap a spoonful of the ginger cream in the cavity of each pear half and arrange them on the watercress or endive. Serves six.

## GRAPE AND PEAR SALAD

Grape leaves
8 pear halves
6 oz. (175g) cream cheese
4 tablespoonsful double cream
2 lb (900g) seedless grapes
French dressing

Cover individual salad plates with grape leaves. Put half a pear on each plate, cut side down. The pears may be peeled, fresh ones, or tinned, just as you like (tinned ones keep their colour better). Mix the cream and cream cheese and spread generously all over the sides and tops of the pears. Cut the grapes in halves and put them flat side down on the covered pears, close together so that they resemble a bunch of grapes. If possible put a piece of stem in the end of the pear. Serves eight.

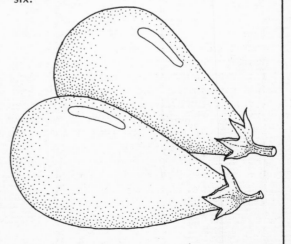

## CITRUS SALAD

1 large lettuce
Little watercress
1 grapefruit, sectioned and peeled
2 oranges, sectioned and peeled
12 dates, stoned
2 oz. (50g) chopped, preserved ginger
3 oz. (75g) cream cheese

Tear the lettuce and watercress into bite-sized pieces and put them in a salad bowl. Add the next 5 ingredients and moisten lightly with citrus dressing. Crumble the cream cheese into the bowl on the top. Serves four or five.

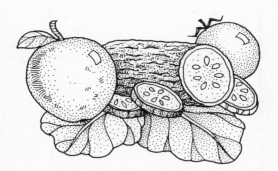

## PEARS WITH FILBERT AND CHEESE BALLS

3 oz. (75g) minced filberts
8 oz. (225g) cream cheese
Pinch of salt
3 dessertspoonsful maraschino cherry juice
8 fresh pears or 16 halves of tinned pears
   (about 2 large tins)
1 cos or salad bowl lettuce

Put the shelled nuts in a shallow baking tin and toast them at 300°F (145°C/Gas Mark 2) until lightly browned. Blend the cream cheese and cherry juice and add the salt then roll into balls the size of small marbles and roll in the minced toasted nuts. Line a large round dish with lettuce leaves and arrange the pear halves on them. If fresh pears are used they must be dipped in lemon juice or they will turn brown. Put some of the cheese-nut balls in the cavities of the pears. Serve with or without french dressing. Serves eight.

## APPLE AND CELERY SALAD

5 oz. (150g) diced apple
5 oz. (150g) tender celery, diced
Salt and pepper, if liked
2 teaspoonsful minced pimiento
1 teaspoonful minced chives
Little lemon and water

Peel and core the apples and dice them then soak in lemon and water then mix all the ingredients together and dress with mayonnaise.

## JELLIED TOMATOES

1 oz. (25g) gelozone
½ pt. (275ml) vegetable stock (light)
3 large tomatoes
1 tablespoonful cooked green peas
1 tablespoonful cooked diced carrot
1 tablespoonful cooked diced chicory
1 large crisp lettuce
1 tablespoonful chopped parsley or chervil

Dissolve the gelozone in the stock. Cut the tomatoes in halves crosswise, scoop out the pulp and seeds, mash the pulp, add to the stock and gelozone and leave in a cold place to set. When it is almost set, add the peas, carrots and chicory and leave until almost firm. Spoon the jelly into the tomato halves, piling it up as high as possible. Serve each tomato on lettuce leaves garnished with parsley or chervil. Serve very cold.

## ARTICHOKE RING

(Use a British Standard Measuring cup for this recipe)

2 cupsful artichoke pulp
1 tablespoonful plain gelozone
¼ cupful cold water
1 level teaspoonful salt
½ cupful french dressing
½ cupful chilli sauce
½ cupful mayonnaise
½ cupful whipped cream
¼ teaspoonful paprika
5 hard-boiled eggs, chopped finely
½ cupful stuffed olives, thinly-sliced

Use globe artichokes for this recipe. Cook them in boiling salted water until tender (about 30 minutes). Drain them well. Remove the leaves and scrape off the tender parts. Chop the hearts and mix with the other pulp. Soak the gelozone in cold water for 5 minutes and then dissolve it over hot water, add the salt, french dressing, chilli sauce, mayonnaise, whipped cream and paprika and mix well with the gelozone.

When blended, stir in the artichoke pulp, eggs and olives and pour into the ring mould which has been rinsed in cold water or lightly oiled, then chill until firm. Turn out on to crisp lettuce and for a luxury salad, fill the centre with pimiento chopped in whipped cream. For more ordinary occasions, a nicely-flavoured potato salad may be used with good effect.

## CRANBERRY RING

1 lb (450g) cranberries
¾ pt. (425ml) cold water
6 oz. (175g) sugar
1 dessertspoonful gelozone
2 oz. (50g) chopped nuts
3 oz. (75g) chopped celery
Lettuce
Mayonnaise

Wash the cranberries and cook them in all but 3 tablespoonsful of the water; cook until they pop. Then add the sugar and cook gently for 5 minutes to melt the sugar. Soften the gelozone in the rest of the water and then dissolve it in the hot mixture adding the salt. Leave to get cool and then chill until it starts to thicken. Fold in the nuts and celery and pour into the ring mould and chill again until firm. Turn out on to a large plate or dish and arrange little bright green lettuce leaves round the ring. You may fill the centre as above. Hand the mayonnaise. A really magnificent effect may be had if the cranberry ring is further garnished with pineapple slices, propped against the sides with a cherry in a blob of stiff mayonnaise in the holes.

## ENDIVE CROWN SALAD

9 oz. (250g) cream cheese
½ teaspoonful salt
10 oz. (275g) drained, grated cucumber
½ pt. (275ml) mayonnaise
3 tablespoonsful minced mild onion
2 oz. (50g) minced parsley
1 clove of garlic, crushed
1 dessertspoonful plain gelozone
3 tablespoonsful cold water
1 head of celery
2 hard-boiled egg yolks, sieved

Rub the garlic round the salad bowl then put the first six ingredients into the bowl. Soften the gelozone in the cold water and dissolve it over hot water, then cool to lukewarm and blend with the first mixture and beat well. Put into a spring form tin, a deep one. Pick over the endive and select sprays of an even height with perfect leaves. Stick whole sprays into the mixture near the sides of the tin to form a close crown, then chill until firm. Remove from the tin on to a bed of lettuce or endive and sprinkle the egg yolk over the top. Garnish with radish roses.

## CHEESE AND TOMATO CROWN

### Red Mould
2 dessertspoonsful gelozone
¼ pt. (150ml) cold water
Large tin of Italian tomatoes
¼ teaspoonful salt, dash pepper
1 bay leaf
1 stalk celery, chopped
1 dessertspoonful vinegar or lemon juice
1 teaspoonful onion juice

Soak the gelozone in the cold water for 5 minutes. Heat the tomatoes, add the seasonings, bay leaf and celery and cook for 10 minutes, over low heat. Strain, add the gelazone, vinegar or lemon juice and the onion juice. Stir until the gelazone is dissolved. Pour into a fluted mould and chill until firm.

## WHITE MOULD

1½ dessertspoonsful gelozone
4 tablespoonsful cold water
1 lb (450g) cottage cheese, sieved
Salt and paprika
¼ pt. (150ml) rich milk

Soften the gelozone in the cold water for 5 minutes. Mix the cheese, salt, paprika and milk. Dissolve the gelozone over hot water then add to the cheese mixture and mix well. Pour into a fluted mould the same size as the red one and chill until firm. Turn out the red mould and the white one and cut each one into the same number of wedges then arrange as one mould alternating the wedges. Garnish with watercress, lettuce or endive.

## MOULDED CHEESE SALAD

1 packet vegetarian lemon jelly
1 pt. (550ml) boiling water
¼ pt. (150ml) cream, whipped
5 oz. (150g) chopped nuts
4 oz. (100g) grated sharp cheese
1 small tin crushed pineapple
3 oz. (75g) stuffed olives, sliced
Cooked salad dressing (see page 00)

Dissolve the jelly in the boiling water, leave to cool and then put in the refrigerator until it starts to set then remove from the refrigerator and whip until it is light and fluffy. Fold in the next 5 ingredients. Pour into an oiled or rinsed ring mould and put back to chill until firm. Turn out and fill the centre with the dressing.

## MOULDED CUCUMBER SALAD

1 small cucumber peeled and diced
¼ teaspoonful salt
½ pimiento, diced
½ teaspoonful lemon juice
2 teaspoonsful gelozone
½ pt. (275ml) cream, whipped

Mix the first four ingredients. Soak the gelozone in the cold water for 5 minutes, then dissolve it over hot water, mix with the whipped cream, fold into the first mixture and pour into individual moulds. Chill and serve with lettuce, chicory or endive. Serves four.

## VALENTINE SALAD

2 tablespoonsful gelozone
¼ pt. (150ml) cold water
1 large tin Italian tomatoes
1 dessertspoonful minced onion
½ teaspoonful celery seed
French dressing
3 oz. (75g) cream cheese

Soften the gelozone in cold water. Heat the next seven ingredients together for 15 minutes. Strain the softened gelozone into the hot mixture, add the lemon juice and set aside to cool. Divide between five heart-shaped moulds and chill until firm. Toss the endive with a little of the dressing and arrange it on six salad plates, then put a jellied tomato heart on each one. If you have no heart-shaped moulds, then set the jelly in a shallow tin and cut the hearts with a biscuit cutter. Serves six.

## MOULDED GRAPE SALAD

1 lb (450g) grapes
4 tablespoonsful french dressing
1 pt. (550ml) hot water
3 oz. (75g) lemon jelly
5 tablespoonsful orange juice
3 tablespoonsful lemon juice
1 teaspoonful onion juice
Good pinch of salt
3 oz. (75g) cream cheese
Salad bowl lettuce leaves

Cut the grapes in halves and remove the pips. Put aside 12 of the grapes. Soak the rest in french dressing for half an hour. Drain, and keep the grapes and dressing separately. Pour the very hot water over the lemon jelly and stir until dissolved. Stir in the lemon, orange and onion juice and the salt. Chill until it begins to set. Stir in the marinated grapes then divide between six individual moulds or a 1 quart (1¼l) mould and chill until set. Soften the cream cheese and make it into six balls. Put the grapes on top of the ring or moulds in a ring with a cheese ball in the middle of each ring of grapes. The cheese balls stay in place if they are slightly flattened. Serve on the lettuce and hand the mayonnaise. Serves six.

## BEETROOT AND OLIVE MOULD

6 oz. (175g) lemon jelly squares
½ pt. (275ml) hot water
½ pt. (275ml) cold water
1 lb (450g) tinned beetroot, shredded
12 stuffed olives, chopped
4 tablespoonsful chopped pickled gherkins
1 dessertspoonful onion salt
1 dessertspoonful garlic powder
Lettuce
French dressing

Dissolve the jelly in the hot water then add the cold water. Drain the beetroot (not pickled beets) and shred it. Add the beet liquor to the jelly and chill until it begins to set. Then blend in the olives, pickles and beet and season with garlic and onion. Put in a 6-inch square tin, well rinsed, or into rinsed individual moulds and put in the refrigerator until set. Turn out on to a dish lined with lettuce. Serves eight to ten.

## POTATO SALAD ROLL

1½ lb (675g) boiled new potatoes, cubed
2 oz. (50g) finely-sliced celery
3 tablespoonsful finely-chopped sweet pickle
2 tablespoonsful minced parsley
2 tablespoonsful minced pimiento
4 hard-boiled eggs, chopped
1 dessertspoonful grated onion
Salt
Paprika
1 dessertspoonful lemon juice
Mayonnaise

Mix the first six ingredients together then add the onion, salt, paprika, lemon juice and enough mayonnaise to bind all together. Turn the mixture on to a piece of cooking foil and shape into a roll 8 x 4 x 2½ inches and roll up in the foil. Put in the refrigerator for 24 hours. Unroll to serve and garnish with radish roses or 'ice' the top with stiff mayonnaise and garnish as liked. Cut in slices to serve. Serves eight.

## GOLDEN GLOW SALAD

1 packet lemon jelly
½ pt. (275ml) boiling water
½ pt. (275ml) tinned pineapple juice
Pinch of salt
2 teaspoonsful lemon juice
1 tin of crushed pineapple
5 oz. (150g) raw carrot, grated
3 oz. (75g) chopped nuts

Dissolve the jelly in the boiling water then add the pineapple juice and salt and stir well. Drop in the lemon juice, stir again and leave to become syrupy. When it begins to set, add the crushed pineapple, carrots and nuts and mix again. Put into a mould and into the refrigerator and turn out when quite firm. Use any salad greens. Serves eight.

## ASHVILLE SALAD

1 lb (450g) cream cheese
1 large tin tomato soup
2 tablespoonsful gelozone
¼ pt. (150ml) cold water
Generous pinch of salt
2 small green peppers, seeded and chopped
2 oz. (50g) chopped crisp celery
Mayonnaise
Lettuce

Heat the soup and dissolve the gelozone in it, then add the cream cheese, green pepper, celery and salt and mix really well. Rinse six moulds (individual ones) in water and divide the mixture between them. Chill until firm and then turn out on to lettuce. Serves six.

## AVOCADO MOULD

1 envelope plain gelozone in 3 tablespoonsful cold water
¼ pt. (150ml) hot water
2 British Standard measuring cupsful mashed avocado
1 level teaspoonful salt
1 teaspoonful onion juice
¼ pt. (150ml) whipped cream
¼ pt. (150ml) mayonnaise

Add the soaked gelozone to the boiling water. Fold the cream into the mayonnaise and then fold into the gelozone mixture. Fold in the avocado pulp, salt and put into a damp ring mould then chill until firm. Then turn out on to a dish and serve garnished to taste; lettuce with tomato wedges look good. Sprinkle the lettuce with french dressing to make it glossy. Serves six.

## CORAL SALAD

1 envelope gelozone soaked in 3 tablespoonsful hot water
1 egg, separated
1½ British Standard measuring cupsful creamy mashed potato
1 British Standard measuring cupful strained tomato pulp
Salt and pepper to taste

Separate the egg and beat the yolk into the mashed potato, add the tomato and blend in an electric blender. Put in a strong pan over low heat or better still put the mixture in the top of a double saucepan over hot water until it thickens. Stir constantly. Remove from the heat, add the dissolved gelozone, salt and pepper to taste. Beat the egg white until very stiff and fold into the first mixture. Turn into a dampened mould and chill in the refrigerator until firm.

# Chapter Seven
# SALAD DRESSINGS

However good the ingredients of a salad may be they need something with which to bind them, something to blend the flavours into a harmonious whole.

Possibly the best known of all salad dressings is mayonnaise. Although experienced cooks sometimes flinch at making mayonnaise, it need not be terrifying. It does, however, need patience to make in the conventional way. An electric blender or a small hand operated emulsifier makes a perfect mayonnaise with ease.

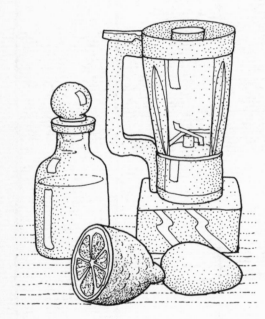

# MAYONNAISE

2 raw egg yolks
½ pt. (275ml) pure olive oil
1 level teaspoonful french mustard
1 heaped eggspoonful salt
1 level eggspoonful freshly ground black pepper
1 dessertspoonful tarragon vinegar *or*
1 dessertspoonful white wine vinegar
Strained juice of ½ small lemon
¼ pt. (150ml) double cream

Chill a bowl. Drop in the egg yolks and the seasonings and mix until they are creamy and blended, then, still beating, add the oil in slow drips until the mixture thickens. Now, but not before, add a few drops of the wine vinegar and the rest of the oil, a little faster than before. Add the remaining vinegar, still beating. Now drop in the lemon juice and lastly the cream. If the mayonnaise is too thick, drop in the other vinegar.

A lighter and more digestable mayonnaise may be made if the egg white is beaten stiffly and folded in just before the mayonnaise is to be used. If in spite of all your care the mayonnaise curdles you can save it by adding a few drops of very hot water in a basin, then add a few drops of the curdled mixture, whisking all the time; add the faulty mayonnaise a little at a time.

# EMULSIFIER MAYONNAISE

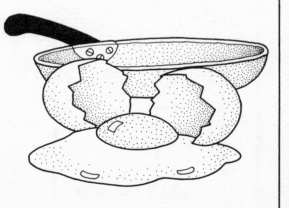

½ pt. (275ml) olive oil
1 level teaspoonful french mustard
1 eggspoonful salt
Dash of pepper
2 dessertspoonsful white wine vinegar
2 raw egg yolks

Put all the ingredients into the emulsifier in the order given and operate it according to the directions on the box. The same method is used for the Electric Blender.

## APPETIZER MAYONNAISE

To ½ pt. (275ml) of the basic mayonnaise add:

½ pt. (275ml) chilli sauce
1 teaspoonful Worcester Sauce
1 teaspoonful prepared horseradish
2 minced pickles
1 stalk of celery, minced
1 dessertspoonful minced chives
2 dessertspoonsful minced parsley

Beat in in the order given.

## BAR-LE-DUC MAYONNAISE

To basic mayonnaise add:

3 tablespoonsful redcurrant jelly
1 dessertspoonful lemon juice

## CHEESE MAYONNAISE

To basic mayonnaise add:

3 oz. (75g) cream cheese
2 tablespoonsful Camembert cheese

Blend well. Especially good with potato or egg salads.

## CREAM CHEESE MAYONNAISE

To basic mayonnaise add:

3 oz. (75g) cream cheese
1 dessertspoonful lemon juice
2 tablespoonsful chopped toasted almonds
6 tablespoonsful whipped cream

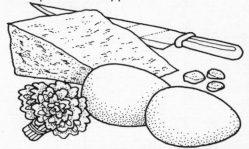

## FLUFFY HORSERADISH MAYONNAISE

To basic mayonnaise add:

6 tablespoonsful whipped cream
3 tablespoonsful prepared horseradish
4 drops Tabasco sauce

## THOUSAND ISLAND MAYONNAISE

Add to ½ pt. (275ml) of basic mayonnaise:

4 tablespoonsful chilli sauce
2 dessertspoonsful chopped stuffed olives
1 teaspoonful chopped capers
1 teaspoonful chopped chives

## TARTARE SAUCE

This is a mayonnaise made from the yolks of hard-boiled eggs. Whisk the yolks to a smooth paste, using the yolks of 4 eggs. Mix in a good pinch of salt and a few drops of vinegar. Pepper may be added to good effect. Press out the juice of a finely-grated onion into a basin and add $\frac{3}{4}$ pt. (425ml) of olive oil in the same way as for basic mayonnaise, that is, drop by drop. Mix and add a few snipped chives.

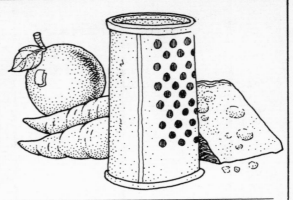

## MAYONNAISE WITHOUT OIL

2 tablespoonsful flour
$1\frac{1}{2}$ teaspoonsful dry mustard
1 teaspoonful salt
Good dash of pepper
2 teaspoonsful sugar
1 tablespoonful melted margarine
1 raw egg yolk, beaten
$\frac{1}{4}$ pt. (150ml) milk
2 tablespoonsful vinegar
1 egg white, whisked

Mix the flour, salt, mustard, pepper and sugar. Put into the top of a double sauce-pan. Mix well and then add the melted margarine, beaten egg yolk, milk and vinegar and whisk. Now put the top of the saucepan over hot water and stir or whisk until the mixture thickens. Take off the heat, cover and leave to cool; then fold in the stiffly beaten egg white and put in a cold place in a covered jar. This is a perfect dressing for those who cannot take oil.

## MAYONNAISE WITHOUT EGG

1 small old potato
1 level teaspoonful made mustard
2 teaspoonsful vinegar
$\frac{1}{4}$ pt. (150ml) olive or salad oil

Steam the potato in its jacket, then peel and mash it. Add the mustard and salt to taste and very slowly the vinegar and beat vigorously then drop in the oil a little at a time. Ideal for those who are allergic to eggs.

## BOILED SALAD DRESSING

1 teaspoonful plain flour
1 teaspoonful dry mustard
Salt, pepper and sugar to taste
1 whole egg, beaten
2 tablespoonsful salad oil
1 pt. (550ml) boiling water
Vinegar

Put the flour and mustard into a small basin, mix and add the pepper, salt and sugar and mix again. Add the beaten egg and when well blended, add the salad oil. Now add the boiling water very slowly, stirring all the time and then add a little vinegar. Put the basin over boiling water or do all the operation in the top of a double saucepan. Cook and stir until the mixture thickens.

## AMERICAN SALAD DRESSING

1 level teaspoonful salt
1 level teaspoonful dry mustard
2 level teaspoonsful sugar
3 dessertspoonsful flour
1 raw egg, beaten
3 dessertspoonsful melted butter or margarine
½ British standard measuring cupful milk
¼ British standard measuring cupful vinegar

Put the salt, mustard, sugar and flour in the top of a double saucepan, add some pepper if liked. Beat the egg and add it and stir all together. Soften the butter or margarine and mix it in then stir in the milk and cook over hot water until thickened. Remove from the heat and drop in the vinegar very slowly, and beat well. Strain and leave to cool. Bottle and cover tighly.

## SALAD DRESSING (1)

2 teaspoonsful cornflour
1 saltspoonful each salt, pepper, sugar and dry mustard
¼ pt. (150ml) water
½ oz. (15g) margarine
1 raw egg yolk
Vinegar to taste

Mix the first five ingredients and blend with the water then put in a saucepan and stir until the mixture boils. Take off the heat and add the margarine, raw egg yolk and whisk well, then drop in vinegar to taste.

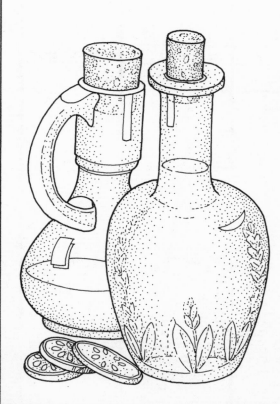

## SALAD DRESSING (2)

½ pt. (275ml) white sauce of coating thickness, well flavoured
1 tablespoonful vinegar
1 saltspoonful each of salt, pepper, sugar and dry mustard

Beat the vinegar into the white sauce. Mix together the salt, pepper, sugar and mustard and beat into the sauce. Taste and adjust the vinegar if needed.

## SALAD DRESSING WITHOUT OIL OR EGG (1)

1 tablespoonful sugar
1 level teaspoonful salt
2 teaspoonsful home-made mustard
1 small tin evaporated milk
3 tablespoonsful vinegar

Mix the sugar, salt and mustard in a basin then by degrees add the undiluted tinned milk slowly. Mix well and add the vinegar drop by drop. When well-blended pour into clean dry bottles with screw tops or corks. Will keep for several weeks.

## SALAD DRESSING WITHOUT OIL OR EGG (2)

¾ oz. (20g) margarine
¾ oz. (20g) plain flour
Salt and pepper
½ pt. (275ml) milk
1 tablespoonful melted margarine

Put the first amount of margarine into the top of a double saucepan stir in the flour and season with salt and pepper. Stir in the milk slowly and put the top over hot water and stir until the mixture thickens. Cook for a few minutes to remove the raw taste, stirring all the time. Take off the heat, leave to get cool and then stir in the tablespoonful of margarine, melted and add, drop by drop vinegar to taste.

## COOKED SALAD DRESSING (FOR STORING)

2 oz. (50g) margarine
2 oz. (50g) plain flour
½ oz. (15g) cornflour
1 teaspoonful dry mustard
3½ teacupsful hot, but not boiling, milk
2 level teaspoonsful sugar
1 level teaspoonful salt
1 raw egg, well beaten
Vinegar to taste

Mix the first four ingredients together and stir in the milk. Keep stirring all the time and when mixed, add the sugar and salt. Boil gently, stirring constantly until the mixture thickens and is quite smooth. Take off the heat and cool for some minutes then stir in the egg and cook *very gently* just to reheat but *do not let it boil*. Cover the pan and leave to cool again then drop in vinegar to taste. This dressing keeps extremely well.

## CHUTNEY SALAD DRESSING

To $\frac{1}{2}$ pt. (275ml) salad dressing, add 1 table-spoonful chutney and mix well.

## COTTAGE CHEESE SALAD DRESSING

4 tablespoonsful cottage cheese
$\frac{1}{4}$ pt. (150ml) evaporated milk
$\frac{1}{4}$ pt. (150ml) lemon juice
1 dessertspoonful clear honey
$\frac{1}{4}$ teaspoonful salt
Dash of paprika
1 dessertspoonful chopped chives

Beat all the ingredients together until smooth.

## CHILLI SALAD DRESSING

To $\frac{1}{2}$ pt. (275ml) dressing, add $\frac{1}{2}$ pt. (275ml) chilli sauce, 3 dessertspoonsful vinegar, 3 tablespoonsful Worcester sauce and a heaped teaspoonful chopped garlic or chives.

## WATERCRESS SALAD DRESSING

$\frac{1}{4}$ lb (100g) watercress
1 clove of garlic, mashed
$\frac{1}{2}$ pt. (275ml) salad dressing
Salt, if needed
2 teaspoonsful lemon juice

Put all the ingredients into an electric blender and blend until the watercress is finely minced.

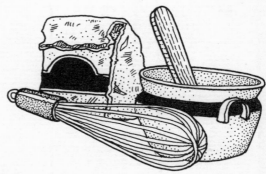

## RED SALAD DRESSING

Tint the dressing with tomato ketchup.

## THREE CHEESES SALAD DRESSING

4 oz. (100g) blue cheese
8 oz. (225g) cream cheese
3 tablespoonsful grated sage cheese
½ teaspoonful fresh tarragon
½ teaspoonful salt
Dash pepper
½ clove of garlic mashed or use granulated garlic
4 tablespoonsful milk

Use your electric mixer for this. Put the cheese in the small bowl of the mixer and mix until well blended. Add the next four ingredients and mix again. Beat in the milk at slow speed until the mixture is like coffee cream. Add enough milk to get this consistency but do not thin too much.

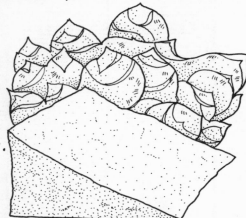

## STANDARD OR BASIC FRESH DRESSING

1 teaspoonful salad
1 saltspoonful pepper
3 tablespoonsful vinegar (wine if possible)
¼ pt. (150ml) olive oil

Mix the dry ingredients and mix in the vinegar, add the oil and shake well before using. Some people like to add a little fine sugar and lemon juice instead of vinegar. Always shake well before use.

## ZIPPY FRENCH DRESSING

½ teaspoonful salt and dash pepper
¼ teaspoonful dry mustard
1 teaspoonful Worcester sauce
1 tablespoonful finely-minced onion
1 clove of garlic or granulated garlic
2 tablespoonsful wine vinegar
6 tablespoonsful olive or salad oil

Mix all the ingredients together and beat with an egg whisk until blended. Must be shaken before use.

## CUP FRENCH DRESSING

1 British standard measuring cupful of salad or olive oil
¼ British standard measuring cupful of vinegar
½ teaspoonful of salt
A few grains of pepper
2 tablespoonsful of chopped parsley

Mix the ingredients together and shake well before use.

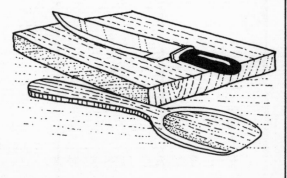

## CAPER FRENCH DRESSING

Add 3 tablespoonsful to basic french dressing.

## TARRAGON FRENCH DRESSING

Use tarragon vinegar instead of plain vinegar in basic french dressing.

## CHIFFONADE FRENCH DRESSING

Add 1 dessertspoonful each of chopped cooked beets, chopped chives and hard-boiled eggs to basic french dressing.

## VINAIGRETTE

Add 1 tablespoonful chopped chives, 1 tablespoonful chopped sweet pickle to basic french dressing.

## FINES HERBES FRENCH DRESSING

Add 1 dessertspoonful each of minced parsley, watercress, chervil and basil to basic french dressing.

## CITRUS DRESSING

Take a covered jar and put in it 4 oz. (100g) castor sugar, 4 tablespoonsful each of tarragon vinegar and tomato ketchup, 1 level teaspoonful salt, 1 small onion, 1 minced clove garlic and about $\frac{1}{2}$ pt. (275ml) salad oil. Cover and shake. Chill before use.

## LOW CALORIE FRENCH DRESSING

$\frac{1}{2}$ pt. (275ml) cider vinegar
1 tablespoonful tomato ketchup
2 tablespoonsful light brown sugar
1 tablespoonful chilli sauce
3-4 tablespoonsful water
$\frac{1}{2}$ teaspoonful minced garlic
$\frac{1}{2}$ teaspoonful dry mustard
$\frac{1}{4}$ teaspoonful each of paprika and black pepper
1 saltspoonful salt

As there is no oil in the dressing this will appeal to weight-watchers. Just put all the ingredients into a jar and shake well.

## LEMON FRENCH DRESSING

¼ pt. (150ml) salad or olive oil
¼ pt. (150ml) lemon juice
¼ teaspoonful salt
Dash of pepper
2 dessertspoonsful clear honey

Put all the ingredients into a jar and shake well.

## LIME FRENCH DRESSING

Use lime juice instead of lemon juice.

## JANE'S SESAME SEED DRESSING

½ teaspoonful salt
2 cloves of garlic
½ pt. (275ml) olive or salad oil
¼ pt. (150ml) vinegar
¼ pt. (150ml) double cream
1 dessertspoonful sesame seeds
Pepper (if liked)

Chop the garlic and mix with the salt then mix all the ingredients together and shake in a large jar. Leave overnight so that the flavours may blend. Excellent over any cabbage salad.

# Chapter Eight
# SUGGESTED MENUS

A very important task for every cook is the arrangement of menus. Not only must the food taste good: it must also look good and tempting and it must be nourishing and well-balanced.

The following menus are only suggestions because many things must be taken into consideration: the availability of the foods, personal likes and dislikes and the amount in the housekeeping purse.

Many of the menus are interchangeable, such as potatoes cooked in other ways than those suggested; another green vegetable substituted for the one given; other foods added, such as potatoes or pasta where neither is given and extra vegetables to serve with the main dish; cheese and biscuits may be served at the end of the meal, and so on.

Many people will prefer a green or mixed salad to a hot vegetable, even in the winter. Remember that if any meal seems short of protein, a hearty soup, or a cheese sauce or one with chopped nuts or grated nuts may be added.

## MENU 1

Creamed celeriac (p. 49)
Poached eggs (with or without cheese
    sauce)
Baked potatoes
Fruit in season

## MENU 2

Breadcrumb omelette (p. 24)
Beets in cranberry sauce (p. 42)
Steamed date pudding (p. 91)

## MENU 3

Nut rissoles with gravy (p. 86)
Baked cabbage with apples (p. 45)
Marshmallow and mint custard (p. 96)

## MENU 4

Spring soup (p. 20)
Sweet corn batter cakes (p. 52)
Green vegetables with grated cheese
Ginger sponge pudding (p. 94)

## MENU 5

Tomato juice
Curried Tomatoes with Herbs (p. 80)
Rice
French or runner beans
Date and orange flan (p. 92)

## MENU 6

Half a grapefruit
Asparagus pie (p. 36)
Mixed salad
Apples baked with geranium leaves (p. 89)

## MENU 7

Vegetable stew with pinwheel top (p. 83)
Globe artichokes vinaigrette (p. 33)
Green salad
Bakes pears and cardamon (p. 90)

## MENU 8

Bakes lasagne (p. 68)
Broccoli salad
Sliced tomatoes
Lemon-scented baked custard (p. 96)

## MENU 9

Bortsch (p. 12)
Pancakes filled with nuts (p. 85)
Kale with cheese sauce (p. 55)
Gooseberry and saffron shortcake (p. 99)

## MENU 10

Cream of celery soup (p. 13)
Carrot and orange *soufflé* (p. 48)
Grapefruit and lettuce cup salad (p. 131)
Fresh fruit or cheese and biscuits

## MENU 11

Fresh green pea soup (p. 16)
Moulded cheese salad (pp. 113, 136)
Yorkshire treacle tart (p. 100)

## MENU 12

Eggs with polenta (p. 27)
New carrot and onion salad (p. 119)
Suppertime ginger pudding (p. 99)

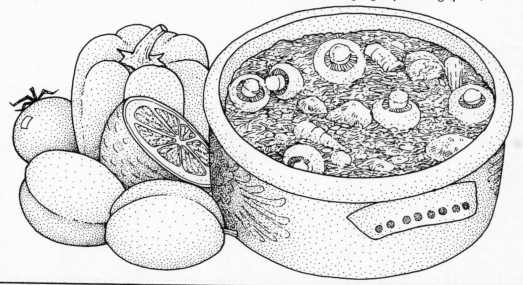

# Food Values of Vegetables

|  | Calories | Protein (g) | Fat (g) | Carbohydrate (g) |
|---|---|---|---|---|
| Artichokes | 135 | 12.4 | .2 | 5.7 |
| Asparagus | 95 | 10.0 | .9 | 17.7 |
| Aubergines | 111 | 4.3 | .8 | 21.7 |
| Beans (lima) | 580 | 34.1 | 3.6 | 106.7 |
| Beans (french/runner) | 159 | 10.9 | .9 | 295.0 |
| Beets | 190 | 7.3 | .5 | 43.5 |
| Beet greens | 123 | 9.1 | 1.4 | 26.4 |
| Beet spinach | 123 | 9.1 | 1.4 | 26.4 |
| Broccoli | 132 | 15.0 | .9 | 25.0 |
| Brussels sprouts | 213 | 20.0 | 2.3 | 40.8 |
| Cabbage | 109 | 6.4 | .9 | 24.0 |
| Carrots | 191 | 5.5 | 1.4 | 42.2 |
| Cauliflower | 114 | 10.9 | .9 | 22.3 |
| Celery | 82 | 5.9 | .9 | 16.8 |

|  | Calories | Protein (g) | Fat (g) | Carbohydrate (g) |
|---|---|---|---|---|
| Chard (Swiss) | 82 | 5.5 | .8 | 17.2 |
| Cucumber | 55 | 3.2 | .5 | 12.3 |
| Dandelion greens | 200 | 12.3 | 3.2 | 40.0 |
| Endive | 91 | 7.3 | .9 | 18.2 |
| Garlic | 450 | 4.4 | .2 | none |
| Kale | 182 | 17.7. | .2 | none |
| Kholrabi | 73 | 5.1 | .2 | 16.4 |
| Leeks | 204 | 10.1 | 1.4 | 46.8 |
| Lettuce | 68 | 5.5 | .9 | 13.2 |
| Mustard greens | 74 | 7.6 | 1.0 | 13.2 |
| Onions (spring) | 204 | 4.5 | .9 | 48.1 |
| Onions (large) | 204 | 6.4 | .9 | 46.7 |
| Parsley | 225 | 16.8 | 4.5 | 49.9 |
| Parsnips | 277 | 5.3 | 1.8 | 64.4 |
| Peas | 445 | 30.4 | 1.8 | 80.4 |
| Peppers (green) | 204 | 4.5 | .9 | 48.1 |
| Potatoes | 375 | 9.1 | .5 | 86.8 |
| Radishes | 91 | 5.4 | .5 | 19.0 |
| Swedes | 147 | 4.2 | .4 | 34.4 |
| Spinach | 91 | 10.4 | 1.4 | 14.5 |
| Summer Vegetable Marrow | 73 | 2.7 | .5 | 17.7 |
| Sweet Corn | 418 | 16.8 | 5.5 | 93.1 |

|               | Calories | Protein (g) | Fat (g) | Carbohydrate (g) |
| ------------- | -------- | ----------- | ------- | ---------------- |
| Sweet potatoes | 558     | 8.2         | 3.2     | 126.5            |
| Tomatoes      | 91       | 4.5         | 1.4     | 18.2             |
| Turnips       | 145      | 5.0         | 1.9     | 32.2             |
| Turnip greens | 136      | 13.2        | 1.8     | 24.5             |
| Watercress    | 84       | 7.7         | 1.4     | 15.0             |

These values are on the basis of 1 lb (454g) edible portion.

# List of Recipes

## PUDDINGS

## TEATIME RECIPES

## SALADS

## SALAD DRESSINGS